Adoption A

From Self-Loathing to Self-Loving

JoJo Miracle Patience

ISBN: 978-1-5272-2563-3

Publisher Information

JoJo Miracle Patience
11 Temple Close
Barnwood
Gloucester
GL4 3ER

jojompatience@gmail.com

A catalogue record of this book is available at the British Library

When blades of grass caress but don't cut

When cold snow melts my pain

When hot sands cauterise my wounds

When water washes and revives

Then is the time I know

I have no need for shoes

JoJo 5th of June, 2003

Dedication

This book is dedicated with unconditional love to my three incredible children **Chris**, **James** and **Lucy**. Thank you each for your wonderful inner and outer beauty. I am so very proud of each of you for your unique amazing gifts and talents and for the way you each show and share love with me.

You are life's most precious gift to me.

Acknowledgments

I wish to personally thank the following people for their support, inspiration, friendship and love in writing this book.

Brett Moran, my best friend, author, yoga teacher and transformational coach, thank you for your belief in me as a writer with a story to share. Heart to heart hugs and love to you. You have inspired and motivated me more than you can imagine. You nudged me, you told me straight and offered me help when you knew I needed it. You saw through my defences, gave me tough love and saw my potential. I don't believe this book would be written and published without you. **Buntie,** my birth mother, thank you for giving me life and for loving me. You are a beautiful woman, and I love you deeply. You have helped me understand the meaning of unconditional love. **Reverend Daniel Burton**, you helped me enormously when I was searching for my birth records. You were there when I really needed a good friend to support me. **Neil Hornsby,** my amazing friend and confidante, you saw me through my lows and highs. You were such an inspiration to me, and I thank you. I will always love you. My friend **Paul "Stalkie" Stalker**, business coach and motivational speaker, I thank you for pulling me aside and telling me to raise my game and re-awakening my quest for self-actualisation. **Mark Cross,** my best friend of the last few years, thank you for the belief that I can do whatever I want. Thank you for caring about me, even though I'm exasperating most of the time. My adopted brother **Jason,** thank you for being you. I love you with all my being.

Much appreciation goes to TV personalities, Nicky Campbell (BBC Long Lost Families), Louis Emerick (Coronation Street), Sian Williams (BBC News) and Mike Leigh OBE (Oscar nominated and BAFTA award winning film producer) for your words of encouragement to me which have boosted me greatly.

Finally, thank you to my late adoptive parents Philip and Daphne. You loved me in your own way. You did what you did through love, and I have become the woman I am as a result.

Contents

Introduction

Once upon a time, I was a princess… That's a total fabrication. I was never a princess. I just imagined that I might have been, but once upon a time seems so long ago now.

"Do you ever want to trace your real mum?" A friend, who was also adopted, asked me one day.

"Of course, I do," I replied, not committing myself to when that might actually be. I had always wanted to know who she was. Why wouldn't I? It seemed only natural to me that I'd get to meet her one day. It was my inherent right to know her. I had made up thousands of stories about her in my head. I had imagined that I might be the love child of someone in the Royal Family, a princess no less. This startling assumption was influenced by my favourite fairy tale from Hans Christian Andersen 'The Princess and The Pea'. Whilst I never actually slept on 20 mattresses and felt the discomfort of a small pea underneath them all, I did hate creases or lumps in a bed and imagined that if I did have 20 mattresses, I would surely feel the pea. This

was proof enough to me that my 'real' mother could well be someone very grand indeed. I knew very little about my birth mother except that she was 23 years old and had been unable to keep me. I romanticised about her and about my beginnings. I had created a fairy tale around these things and believed that one day I would live my very own happily ever after. My friend had the polar-opposite perspective to me.

"Why the hell would I want to ruin the completely wonderful life that I have by meeting someone who means nothing to me?" She did not romanticise anything, it seemed.

"Don't you ever think about her, or wonder what she might be like?" I questioned her. "Don't you ever consider who she might be? She might actually be someone famous!" I exclaimed, as if this would make a difference to how my friend would respond. She was adamant that it was not even remotely possible that she would ever search for her birth mother. She believed it would betray her adoptive parents, who had given her a brilliant life and loved her dearly.

"I'm not even telling my mum and dad I'm looking" I told her indignantly. "It has absolutely nothing to do with them. This is about me." It was true. I had no intention of sharing any of my search with them. I felt quite strongly that this was my own quest for truth and not something I needed to share. It was something I could do on my own, for me because I wanted to and not because someone had told me to. I honestly believed that my adoptive parents, more specifically my adoptive mother, would not understand and would in some way see my need to know as a personal slight. I felt that my adoptive mother might even try to veto my decision. It wasn't a risk I was willing to take.

"You're being totally disrespectful and dishonest," my friend accused.

"I don't give a flying fuck."

****

****

You are probably holding this book right now as an adoptee or someone interested in the issues around adoption. Many adoptees are still struggling to feel good about their adoption. They are fractured, traumatised and looking for answers. For some, there is a deep pervading pain and an overwhelming sense that the foundations of their world have been irreparably damaged.

If you're an adoptee, do you ever find yourself feeling so overwhelmed by your adoption that you're disconnected from yourself and everyone else? Do you wonder about your birth family and what life might have been like if you had stayed with them? Or maybe you need some help with working through how you really feel about being adopted? I know that, for me, these things were true for many years. I have gone from self-loathing to self-loving, and it's not been the smoothest of rides that's for sure. I don't claim that this book will change your life. After all, it is simply a collection of paper and words. What I do know is that I am personally in a good place physically, mentally and spiritually now and that is not a fluke. It's been a concerted effort to change.

I've practised my own personal alchemy, if you like, and I hope that this book may help you to do the same.

On a really good day, you may find that you read something here and have a light bulb moment that takes you off on an interesting journey. On a really bad day, where your adoption story has got its claws into you, you may just want to wallow in self-pity and throw this book in the bin. That's partly the reason I wrote this book for you (not so you can throw it in the bin obviously!), because I've had days just like that, bad, terrible days. And, I've also had great ones. The very knowledge of being adopted weaves itself into the core of our personalities like out of control bindweed on a mountainside attaching itself to us, often smothering us in the process. That knowledge, unless well managed, can be pernicious and affect how we think and behave throughout our entire lives.

Once, whilst trekking in the Himalaya in India, after the hardest and steepest of climbs I found that I had been rewarded with the best view I'd ever seen. My life, up until this point, has been a progressive journey that at times felt like an insurmountable mountain to climb. Though the climb has been broken by plateaus that gave me time to breath and take stock of where I was, often I ended up taking a totally wrong turn and falling into the brambles. And as I nursed my scratches, I would wallow in the pain of being lost. But there always came a time, a place or a person that helped me get back on the right path. The summit seemed so far away, so damn hard to reach, but little by little it came into view more clearly. It became bigger, bolder and brighter, and as I neared the top a tremendous sense of both wonder and expectation gave me the boost I needed to make it.

While my personal adoption journey will be different from yours I truly hope that my words and experiences will inspire you to take the action you need to change how you feel. I've thrown in a few tips and strategies that have worked for me and that you, too, might find useful. If you're an adoptee that is in a great place and happy with the world, then I applaud you. I am certain there will be parts of the book that resonate with you deeply. If, on the other hand, you are an adoptee struggling to see how you'll ever reach the top of your personal mountain, then read on because you will learn how to deeply love yourself. You will discover that your adoption doesn't have to define you and that in order to feel a deep joy inside yourself, there are some simple actions you can take to feel so much better. This book is mostly based around my personal reflections and experiences of being adopted as a baby, following relinquishment and my subsequent healing journey. Of course, this doesn't negate the experiences of anyone adopted as an older child or under any different circumstances, and many of the feelings, beliefs and behaviours are much the same. I feel that the exercises are as valid for anyone in the adoption triad as they are for adoptees.

I told my story publicly for the first time when, in 2010, I was interviewed for BBC Radio, broadsheet newspapers and a couple of magazines for a piece on adoption as part of UK National Adoption Week. I got a couple of speaking engagements as a result, and it seemed like people wanted to listen to my story. The more people asked, the more I was able to articulate my story in a way that acknowledged my feelings and those of other adoptees, which helped me recognise that sharing my story was a catalyst for change in myself and others. This book is mainly for people who are adopted, however, anyone with an interest in families, relationships and the human condition will get something from it, too. The challenges, behaviours and emotions in the book are common to many people from all different backgrounds and so I share what has worked in my life to move me from a place where I didn't like myself very much to one where I, now, fully embrace the woman that I am.

Adoption affects each person differently at different stages of life. You are totally unique, and no one will have travelled the same journey or walked in your exact shoes. However, there are certain commonalities that adoptees often share, and it is these that this book seeks to address. These are the issues that I have faced, and I will offer a perspective on how I have dealt with them that may help you as well. Of course, *Adoption Alchemy* is just one book that documents my personal adoption experiences and what actions I took to change. How you respond to what you read is totally up to you. My dearest wish is that you feel as happy as I do right now because you deserve to be happy. This is a book that is more than just an adoption self-help book: it is a way of living inside yourself so that you feel deeply connected to your own inner magic and beauty.

I have written this from a deep place of self-love in my heart. I have learned over the years that we are less likely to be able to help others unless we can practice self-love. I firmly believe that when we each start to crack open our hearts and face the demons and darkness that can sometimes overwhelm us, only then can we allow true healing. If you cultivate the tools needed to change and stop resisting them, then you can truly perform your own personal adoption alchemy. So please, come with me on a journey and let's see where it takes us. I recommend treating yourself to a journal or diary so that you can document your journey, your thoughts and the exercises that I will walk you through.

Let us begin.

Chapter 1

Awareness

So, You're Adopted

A child born to another woman calls me mom. The depth of the tragedy and the magnitude of the privilege are not lost on me. — Jody Landers

I was three years old when my daddy told me I was adopted. He was always the one to tuck me in at night and tell me bedtime stories, so it was only natural that he would be the one to tell me this fantastically strange story. I always felt closer to my dad than my mum as I was growing up; he was the one I would have fun with and who made me laugh. Mum was the strict one. The 'bad cop' in their good cop bad cop routine, or at least that's how I thought about it years later. Daddy always smelled of bonfires as he would often burn the garden rubbish in the evening. The smell stuck to his clothes and made my nose twitch. It was a great smell, that smoky bonfire smell, one which I still love to this day. Daddy and I did silly things together and I would giggle as he tried to get me to say tongue twisters. "Peter Piper picked a peck of pickled peppers," I tried hard to say it, failing miserably every time. I had no idea what a peck of pickled peppers was, but I'd roll about the bed laughing in total frustration at not being able to say it. I felt so safe and loved with him.

"You are going to have a baby brother soon," my daddy announced one bedtime. I was beyond excited—I loved babies. I knew my aunt was having a baby and I asked why her tummy was getting fat and Mummy's wasn't. "Well, I'm going to tell you a special story tonight. It's a true story about you," explained my daddy. I loved his stories especially with me in them. Daddy was brilliant at storytelling.

He sat with me on my bed as I snuggled into the crook of his arm. He told me that I was very special because he and my mummy had chosen me to be their baby. He said I was born to another mummy who couldn't look after me, so I was adopted. She had loved me so much that she gave me away so that I could be happy with a new mummy and daddy. I remember a strange feeling deep inside my tummy. I did not know what the word 'adopted' meant, *but I grew up with it fixed in my vocabulary. I grew up always knowing that I was adopted. It was an overwhelming thing to hear when I was still so young. I couldn't really make sense of it or understand what he was saying. I remember looking at his face as he held me close and I saw his eyes water. He kept saying that he and my mummy loved me. I knew even at that age that what he told me was something big. I remember imagining having another mummy somewhere and feeling sad at the thought.*

****

****

I think that being told you are adopted is one of the single most overwhelming things for a small child to comprehend. It's such a paradoxical situation. Many of us are told, "Y*our birth mother loved you so much that she gave you away for the chance of a better life.*" Being exposed to such a contradictory message at an early age leaves a lasting legacy on your deeper self—a sort of imprint or echo, which, rather like a tattoo, stays with you and can become distorted as you grow up.

We are seen as little miracles for an individual or couple unable to conceive naturally. Some may grieve the loss of the possibility of becoming natural parents. Yet *their* miracle is that they can still be parents and share their lives with a child. Fifty years ago, adoption was seen as a panacea for couples unable to conceive and for unmarried mothers to save face, a perfect quick fix to save the reputation of a young girl and to complete a happy home for a couple longing for a child. Some people however saw adoption as the last resort. "When all else fails there is always adoption." The very idea of being a last resort for couples fills many adoptees with feelings of utter worthlessness. These feelings can be pervasive and remain deeply ingrained in the psyche for a lifetime.

As an adopted child we often feel that we never really belong. We have two families, our birth family and our adopted family, and we are never fully present in either. Our primary relationship experiences come from our caregivers—most often parents. As an adoptee, you feel the loss of your birth mother deeply, and even though many, though not all, of us are lucky enough to find loving adoptive homes the trauma of that loss stays with us. You create an internal belief that those who love you will leave you, leaving a deep emotional wound that is wrapped up in those eternal words, "Your mother loved you so much that she wanted you to have a better life." Isn't a mother's love unconditional? How can it be so if she gave her child away?

As an adoptee, you are faced with a deep conflict early on in life when separated from your birth mother. The natural attachment to your mother is critical to your survival—without her you would die. This attachment sets the whole foundation for your future relationships. If you were a puppy, you would stay with your birth mother for at least six to eight weeks, yet society deems it perfectly acceptable to remove a human baby from her or his mother at birth or within mere days. It is traumatic, and that trauma becomes coded into the baby's nervous system. Adoption author and psychologist Nancy Verrier calls this the 'primal wound'. It is a deep and gaping wound that opens up when a baby is separated from its mother. Over time, the wound festers and becomes infected with fear. Within the wound lies abandonment, sadness, loss, grief, vulnerability and a lack of trust. Nancy writes, "This wound, occurring before the child has begun to separate his own identity from that of the mother, is experienced not only as a loss of the mother, but as a loss of the Self, that core-being of one's self which is the centre of goodness and wholeness."

Self-Check-In

Think about the person you love most in the world. Can you just imagine if you never saw them again? If I try to imagine that, I get this feeling right in the centre of my body, like a vacuum cleaner trying to suck out my soul. How can a baby or small child cope with that feeling? It is all-consuming, overwhelming, numbing and frightening. So how did we cope with it as infants? We had no option but to develop coping mechanisms to protect ourselves. Think about how these coping mechanisms may have affected you into adulthood.

If, like me, you were passed from birth mother to foster carer (or similar) and then onto an adoptive family, this disruption spills over into every aspect of your life. Your internal working model becomes programmed to prepare for survival in an unsafe world. In this situation, you believe the world to be a scary place, you cannot trust your caregivers for fear that they may leave you again. This distrust is beyond your conscious awareness. But you feel stressed by a world of never-ending change and are in a constant state of alarm.

Along with the snippets of DNA, the stresses and emotions of the birth mother (who is likely worrying about giving her baby up for adoption) pass to her unborn child. The mother's dwelling on negative thoughts about the conception, pregnancy, and perhaps the reasons for needing or wanting to give up her child ultimately take their toll on the unborn baby. Stressed before and after birth, you are born into a state of fear.

From the earliest experiences, both pre- and postnatal, the adoptee's brain is conditioned to feel a sense of loss—loss of the birth mother, loss of a sense of belonging and loss of significance. We grow up with a deep sense that something is missing in our lives. Many adoptees try to ignore these feelings of loss, but they often surface when least expected. However, developing more awareness about your preconceived emotions and beliefs around adoption can help you change your own perspective. Even if there are areas in which you really struggle, awareness will help you train your mind so that you are better equipped to deal with your own personal adoption journey. Feeling confused, lonely, unworthy, abandoned or overwhelmed about your adoption can determine how you value yourself. Once we become more aware and the power that these feelings have over us diminishes, we can start to consider that we are far stronger than we had once believed.

****

****

I walked up the aisle of the church feeling self-conscious and a little embarrassed. I was dressed in a light blue dress and dark blue T-bar shoes, which showed off my new ruffle edged white ankle socks. I wore an 18ct gold cross and chain—a gift from my parents on this auspicious occasion. I was 11 years old and was about to be confirmed into the Church of England. The last time I'd walked up the aisle I was 6 years old wearing a salmon pink satin dress that rustled as I walked. Everybody was watching me as I walked up behind the bride. I remember feeling a sense panic and self-consciousness preemptively worrying in case I did something wrong then, too. I wanted to be perfect and for everyone to think the best of me.

This time, I felt anything but perfect because I was the only girl in blue. The others all wore white—pretty, frilly white—white dresses, white socks and white shoes. I wondered if God might think less of me for turning up in blue. I wondered if the parents of the other girls would also think less of me. I certainly thought less of me. My mum though had insisted I wear blue. "It's a ridiculous idea," she remarked, "that anyone should buy a white dress just for one day that you're never going to wear again." I knew then that after that day I never wanted to be seen in this dress again. It was itchy as hell and I felt like a total idiot in it. I didn't feel like I fit in with everyone else. But whatever my mother said went. So, I wore blue—a blue flash of discomfort amidst a sea of calm white.

I stood alongside the other children ready to be confirmed by the Bishop, a representative from God doing God's work. "God?" I asked, not sure if He would hear, "I hope you're ok with me in blue. My mother made me wear it, so please don't hold it against me." I drifted off, half expecting God to speak

to me when I felt the Bishop's hands on my head and his voice quietly saying,

"Joanna, God has called you by name and made you his own." I was giddy as

the potent smell of incense hit my nostrils. I wondered if I ought to feel

anything dramatic at that point, maybe the Holy Ghost 'whooshing' into me,

but there was nothing. If God had called me, I must have missed it. Yet the

Bishop was clear, God had made me his own. I felt queasy. What did that

mean? "God had made me his own." Did I belong to him, was God adopting

me? Anxiously, I wondered, why would God adopt me? I was already

adopted!

****

****

It's funny how our minds work, how the slightest thing can
trigger such strong emotions even resulting in physical
manifestations of those feelings. There was me, in church,
freaking out that God was about to adopt me knowing full well
that I was already adopted. Add that to the anxiety of being the

odd one out (wearing blue) and we have some totally irrational thoughts causing me to feel sick to my stomach.

That was my ego raising its head above the parapet, trying to be helpful and protect me. That's what the ego does, and it does it well. Protecting you is the ego's primary job. The idea of being adopted by God seemed threatening, so my ego stepped in to protect me. Unfortunately, sometimes the ego is rather overprotective, and for adoptees, in particular, the ego attempts to overcompensate for the loss of our birth mother. The ego is a difficult thing to master: it always wants to be in control. It typically attempts to separate us from our surroundings, driving a wedge between you and your connection to the wider universe. The resulting consequence is that you may feel out of sync with other people at times or simply out of sorts in general, often not being able to put your finger on any one thing that is wrong but knowing, somehow, that you do not feel quite right. The ego can lead to a lot of distractions, and if you allow those distractions to persist you may be missing out on so much that life has to offer. I know that well, as for years and years I allowed my ego to run my life. If you can see yourself in this, know that you can control the ego.

11-year-old me, talking in my head to God, felt very embarrassed, embarrassed to be different. The ego felt threatened as my self-esteem took a knock. I definitely felt out of kilter—separate from everyone else around me and distinctly separate from God. Fellow adoptees may well understand this feeling, that moment when you feel totally stressed, tense and overwhelmed in an otherwise simple situation. That is the ego at work. Being told I was adopted led to me feeling embarrassed about being different and anxious about getting something wrong, which laid the foundations for my whole life. Your life reflects what you believe you deserve, and often adoptees do not believe they deserve very much. Your thoughts shape the way you view the entire world. Even though you make changes constantly and expect things to be different, they aren't, are they? That was once deeply true for me. At one point in my life when I felt terribly stuck, I got divorced. For a while, yes, I felt different, but it was only a temporary sugar coating—soon dissolving leaving me feeling just as I had been before. The French novelist Anais Non once said, "You do not see the world as it is, you see it as you are." Now I understand how profoundly true that is.

Awareness is everything. Once you become aware of your internal working model of the world and see your thoughts and beliefs not as permanent fixtures but mutable fittings then you can begin to make radical changes. The first stage in awareness is getting a bit excited for the next step. Believe me when I say that anything is possible. Even though you may be stuck in the trauma and internal dialogue of your adoption, feeling totally worthless, hating yourself and the world, you can still become more aware and create a life that you want and deserve.

Having once been stuck for a very long time I know that by changing my thoughts I can change my world. I am living proof that this method works. I have done it and continue to do so in my life. I would love for you to feel the change as well, because knowing that you have this opportunity the alternative does not warrant thinking about.

You can either fall down the rabbit hole of powerlessness and heartache or become the creator of your own life. Now that you know the options, you have the power to make the choice.

****

****

Chapter 1 Personal Alchemy Exercise

The following exercise will help you to focus and start you off on your personal alchemic journey. In order to begin to create the life you really want, you first must deconstruct the view of the world that you have already created. It is not doing you any good as it is. With every new thought you have, you are creating your future. It is simple logic, to create a positive future you must start with positive thoughts. To do so, you are going to begin by asking yourself some questions. Questions are a great way to help you change naturally rather than just telling yourself to do something, or even just thinking about yourself differently is a good start. If you catch yourself thinking negatively about yourself (we all do it, me included) instead of dwelling on that negativity, ask how you could tweak it to become a question and not a statement of fact. This will fire up the problem-solving part of your brain. Thoughts lead to words, which lead to action and finally habits.

Ask yourself these 8 questions now, write them down, say them aloud, or just consider them internally:

- Am I ready to change my thoughts and, therefore, my life?
- What is the worst thing that can happen?
- Are the thoughts I'm having true? (You'll work on these in Chapter 5 as well.)
- Are my thoughts giving me power or taking it away?
- Is there a specific issue I need to address?

- Is my life going forwards or backwards?

- What have I done to contribute to how I think and feel?

- Who am I being right now?

Be really honest with yourself when you answer these questions. No one else will see your answers; this is purely for you to start to dig a little deeper into yourself.

When you have completed the questions, check in with yourself. How are you feeling right now?

Chapter 2

Loss

Oh, Mother Where Are You?

The loss for the adoptee is unlike other losses we have come to expect in a lifetime, such as death and divorce. Adoption is more pervasive, less socially recognized, and more profound. — Dr. David M. Brodzinsky and Dr. Marshall D. Schechter

I pushed my way into this world prematurely, weighing less than two bags of sugar, on Monday the 18th of March at Alexandra Park Nursing Home in Muswell Hill north London to a 23-year-old unmarried nursery nurse. I may not consciously remember the moment that my birth mother gave me up, but I am certain I would have cried with despair. The woman who had carried me for nine months everywhere she went was suddenly not there when I needed her most. I was just a little baby screaming in desperation for my mother to return and soothe me at her breast as only she would be able. I wonder how long I screamed, how long I waited until I realised that she was not coming back. There is nothing quite so sad and heart rending as hearing a baby crying desperately for their mother.

After a brief spell in hospital I was passed to foster carers until a suitable adoptive family could be identified. "The baby is a funny little thing," noted my birth records. "She is not thriving very well and has a crumpled ear and a rather startled look." I really did sound like the puppy no one would want to take home. It's hardly surprising that I had a startled look—I had been taken from my mother and placed in an environment that was totally alien to me, with new smells, new voices, new sounds and new experiences. Babies might not be able to speak but they know when something isn't right. I knew. It was decided that until I was thriving better it would be best not to offer me up for adoption. After all, no one would want a 'faulty' baby. Yet at the age of 4 months, I was placed into my forever home with my new adoptive parents. A cute, innocent, happy smiling baby helping to create the perfect family for a perfect happily ever after story.

****

****

Adoption is seen as a beautiful, joyous occasion for the adoptive family. This can be such a conflicting message—joy around loss. It is terribly one sided and fails to consider what the baby or child might be experiencing. Outwardly, as a newly adopted baby, I was all smiles. But inside, at a subconscious level, I was grieving the loss of my birth mother, and it was utterly overwhelming. It seems to me that many adoptive parents view the adoption date as the beginning of a baby's life, completely forgetting that there may have been weeks or months of that child's life prior to the adoption. It is a 'new beginning'.

It is sometimes said that adoption is not all rainbows and unicorns. There is always a story before adoption, a story of loss and sadness, a story of trauma and tumultuous struggle. Loss is a pivotal piece of the adoption mechanism, and this type of loss is unlike any other experienced. The grief that comes with it is immense; it can stay with you for an entire lifetime while resolution seems impossible. It can feel like you are stuck on the fairground roller coaster. It might seem bearable at first, but after a while you want it to stop, to get off and feel the earth beneath your feet. You want to feel secure and safe. You want your mother's arms to wrap around you in a never-ending hug—the sort of hug that only a mother can give. Unfortunately, no one told the roller coaster operator that and so the ride just keeps on going. And finally, when it does come to a stop your mind is so churned up, so shaken that it cannot focus on anything except the awful experience it just endured. You relive it time and time again. For many adoptees, myself included, the grief and loss of my birth mother was never addressed. It just was not something anybody considered. After all, I was a tiny baby adopted into a loving home. What did I know of grief or loss? Babies don't remember anything, do they?

But there is absolutely no getting away from it: adoption involves loss. The loss of your birth family and, in particular, your birth mother is dramatic. The effect of that loss stays with you all through your life and, unless you do something about it, can be terribly damaging. At times, I felt overwhelmed when I had to make a decision about anything, I felt constantly guilty even though I didn't know why. Maybe you felt or feel the same. Guilt is a common feeling for many adoptees and, in fact, for many people that are separated from their natural family or people they love dearly. Adoption loss is in a class of its own. If, for example, a family member dies you have whole rituals around the event: you have the funeral and the wake and are given the opportunity to openly grieve for the loss. These rituals offer closure. Adoption loss can cause you to feel pangs of guilt (for something which isn't your fault anyhow), and there is no apparent closure. Some adoptees feel that they should never have been born or that in some way they, by virtue of being born, are to blame for their birth parents giving them up. I had no idea why I felt guilty; I just knew that I did. It's known as false guilt when we make ourselves feel dreadful about something for no good reason. It's overwhelming, especially when you can't fathom why you even feel like that. For so many adoptees there is still this intrinsic feeling of guilt, for which we seek validation, and it remains part of us for a very long time.

The loss around adoption can be massive. It is the loss of a birth mother and birth family, the loss of identity (we will explore this more deeply in Chapter 6) and the loss of a deep biological connection to the adoptive parents; it can all seem insurmountable. This is not just loss that you feel. It expands and grows, developing a life of its own as it morphs into abandonment and rejection, which in turn leads us to a place of distrust and fear. It affects your future relationships, especially your intimate ones. Would you say that you are 'just fine'? If you are anything like I was before I began my adoption alchemy journey, you are, or at least you say you are. That is the protective wall that your ego has built up around you to keep you safe. Unfortunately, this wall also stops others from getting too close to you. You want to feel close to others and yet you can't help but push them away. I believe that the most deeply motivating factor for this behaviour is the fear of secondary rejection.

Self-Check-In

Do you find that you resist what it is you need the most? I know I did. I acted out my grief and loss in ways that challenged my parents and even as an adult challenged those who loved me most. Consider if you may have ever taken your grief out on others. How has that affected your life?

Rejection is the nemesis of all adoptees, myself included. You believe you did something wrong by being adopted and therefore you want to mitigate the potential for any other rejection later on in life. The loss and rejection are personalised by adoptees, as well as the resulting guilt that somehow, we were to blame. You may fear telling people that you feel overwhelmed, lost, sad or needy, believing that it might just push them away from you and you cannot risk that rejection. So, maybe it is better to say, "I'm fine." When in fact you feel completely overcome with emotion. I can honestly tell you that this strategy is not at all sustainable. Well, unless you want to feel miserable and stuck in your own adoption story for your entire life. I was stuck in mine for fifty years before I became more acutely aware of my thoughts, behaviour and feelings and how I could actually change them. The feelings of rejection and personal responsibility go hand in glove with loss but let me tell you something right now: you are most definitely not to blame.

Someone once said that if you do not first become lost, you can never be found. So, whilst being lost can, at times, be scary and overwhelming, it can also lead to liberation and a deeper understanding of who you are.

****

****

As a child, and even as an adult, I was constantly striving to be perfect and failing miserably. I felt that my life was worth less than those who were not adopted. I saw my friends and assumed they were happier than me, that they had nicer parents, better clothes and more exciting holidays. I spent a good deal of time staring out of the bedroom window at people going past while wondering what their lives were like. I always thought everyone else was better than me. The more I told myself that I wasn't any good, the more that materialized in my life—not doing that well at school, failing my eleven-plus exam, being promiscuous as a teenager, smoking cigarettes, using recreational drugs and trying to constantly people please.

I decided that I could continue to feel a deep sadness and discomfort, or I could make a change and stop allowing my story to define me. But at this point I was already so wrapped up in my story that I didn't even realise it was one. It was just me. That is how it was at that time: it was my only truth. However, there comes a point in life where you have a decision to make. I got to that point in my early 50's after nearly half a lifetime of allowing my story to disempower me to the point of feeling like a lesser human. I tried hard to be amazing and perfect. I tried too hard and failed. Something was holding me back, stopping me from thriving and reaching my potential. I had to find out how I could start to feel different. I'd had enough of being controlled by my story. The 'poor me' victim kept playing over and over and, like a recurring dream, I just could not seem to move on.

I read a pile of self-help books and articles on adoption loss and tried to take the action that was suggested, but something was still stopping me. I knew I wanted to change my story but really could not see to do so. I remember once lying in bed asking myself what I needed to let go of that was not contributing to a positive life experience: it was my thoughts about my adoption and all the associated behaviour around loss. I tried so hard not to be a victim in my story. I tried so hard to let it go. But my story itself did not want to change. It had taken a life of its own and was the strongest influencer on everything I did. It was like a leech; it wasn't going to let go easily and even if it did, it was not going to feel nice. I felt a real, physical internal struggle as my body didn't want to give up the feelings and beliefs I had about adoption. It was unsettling. I felt it right in my gut, like there were hands inside my body holding back the feelings. It was as though giving them up would be the death of me. But I could not give up. Changing my early story, or at least how I felt about it, came when I least expected it. It was during a transformational coaching session when my amazing coach and now best friend, Brett Moran, led me to explore a new experience. He told me to close my eyes.

"Put your left hand on your heart," he guided me, "and travel down your timeline to that tiny baby, that little Jo. Imagine you are there with her as an observer and connect to her. What does she need? What can you say to her?"

I was there, and I could see her. She looked so sad and alone. She was crying. She was still there living in that moment even though it had been over 50 years. She was stuck in a time warp, part of her there and part of her morphed into me. That small, helpless, scared baby, I gathered her in my arms and hugged her tight. She cried for the loss of her mother, clinging to me in desperation. She seemed confused and in a state of alarm. She needed a deeper love than she had ever before felt. I told her that she was truly loved, that she was not abandoned and that everything would be alright. Her life would turn out fine, and she would be so happy. I never wanted to stop hugging her, and I felt the corners of my eyes begin to dampen.

The fear of abandonment is common in adopted children, and the knowledge that we were once abandoned by our first mother is always there. I did not want to consider that my first mother abandoned me as I believed that abandonment meant she disassociated with me both physically and emotionally. The word abandon is soulless, empty and cold and I could not bear to label myself as abandoned. I could not believe that anyone, let alone a mother, would really, utterly forsake her child. There had to be part of her that was still connected to me, however small, maybe a memory, a smell or a sound that would remind her that deep within both her and her child there would always be a common thread, a soul connection. After all, I had literally been a part of my birth mother for nine months.

In that moment with Brett I realised that for over 50 years I was carrying a belief that I had been abandoned, and my subconscious mind played out that belief in everything I did. But now I had connected to the baby Joanna and reassured her that there would be a happy ending. I think she believed me.

****

****

This simple yet effective process profoundly changed how I feel about loss. I know that it is still there, but it seems somehow different, less painful. I no longer feel so scared when I try to think about it. I believe deeply that on some level the baby Joanna was able to cope with the loss after my current-self had paid her a visit. That may sound a bit far-fetched to some, but time is not so linear in the heart and mind. Anything is possible.

The simple truth is that visiting myself as a baby was a powerful exercise that worked for me. The facts may remain unchanged and the primal wound still open, but my feelings about it no longer choke or overwhelm me as they once did. If you could feel differently about a belief that would benefit you in the long term, then surely it must seem sensible to explore things a little deeper. You might even try travelling down your own timeline to the time just prior to your adoption. Don't be scared: allow yourself to go with it. Just see how it works for you.

I don't believe that the pain and trauma of adoption loss is insurmountable. It might seem that way but, in essence, it is much more easily tackled if you can allow yourself to have an open mind, open heart and a willingness to explore things a little deeper than you have before. I promise you that nothing terrible will happen. How can it? You are in total control of yourself. You can reconcile the pain of the loss of your birth mother. You can change how you feel (you *really* can), and the life you want can be yours. When I came to this realization, I gave up the awful critical self-talk and totally indifferent behaviour and worked on letting my loved ones in. Once I really opened up and stopped resenting the people who tried to help me then I allowed the magic to happen.

It's funny how we are the ones who make things so complicated for ourselves. If I had known then what I know now, my life would have been drastically different. Hindsight is easy; it is through our own past experiences and those of others that we can learn. However, hindsight only becomes insight if we actually learn from it. I have come to realise that unless you take time out to reflect on your past story in a positive way you cannot take your life forward the way you want to. It is in the focused things you do that you will find the most powerful changes. The profound experience of walking down my timeline to the baby Joanna showed me that the answers were inside me all along. It is something only you can do for yourself and it is incredibly empowering. All you need is to reevaluate that story in your head, flip the script and rewrite it.

I repeated the timeline exercise at home alone; I revisited the baby Joanna again as I had done with my coach previously. I saw her with her birth mother. Her mother was holding the tiny baby (me) looking deep into her eyes. Her birth mother looked broken and traumatised. She looked so alone and sad. I told them both that I loved them and hugged my birth mother. I gave her the hug of a daughter, forgiving her for giving me away. I told her we would meet again in the future and that the pain of our separation would diminish. In that moment, I had an epiphany. Being 'given up' was not the paradox I had previously believed. It was the opposite of everything I had been feeling. My birth mother had acted with love and integrity. It was a selfless act of love—unconditional love. And to this day I truly believe that.

****

****

Chapter 2 Personal Alchemy Exercise

The realisation of unconditional love led me to do something else which I think you may find helpful too, whatever your beliefs about your birth mother may be. I wrote to my birth mother as she prepared to give me up. This process of writing a letter, known as transactional writing, is a powerful way to move through your early adoption trauma. It offers an opportunity to see things from a different perspective as you can write from the heart and say whatever it is that you need to say. Writing down how you think and feel and what you believe can all be hugely cathartic and help in your adoption alchemy. It can help to heal the immense loss felt.

This is my letter.

To the woman that nurtured and carried me for nine months,

I guess that right now you are feeling overwhelmed with different emotions. Your world is about to be turned upside down and so is mine. We are about to embark on a tough journey together as we will soon be separated from each other for who knows how long. It may be that we never see each other again. I can feel your pain, your angst and your despair. I don't know the reasons why we will be separated, and I can already sense something dramatic is going to happen soon. I think that I am feeling what you are feeling as you feel it, living it as you live it and coping as you cope.

I will cry for you, I know I shall and you will most probably cry for me. Our voices will be lost in the winds of time and the words scattered like autumn leaves. Deep inside we will each know that the other cries even though we cannot hear each other. I will be comforted by another who is not you but who will try their best to replace you. My hope is that you have someone who will comfort you too. Despair is utterly consuming, and my deepest wish is that neither of us falls into that fathomless chasm. Such a dark hole would surely be the death of us both. We both have so much to bring to the world, we are creatives with our lives still blank canvases. We can each paint whatever picture we wish, and I hope that yours will be bright and beautiful, not sad and dark.

Please know that whatever I say in the future, how I behave and how I feel is my complete responsibility and that I do not hold you accountable for my actions. You have birthed me, and I thank you for that because with each new birth, no matter the circumstance, comes possibility and potential. I will try and live life in a way that will make you proud of me as a human being, your child and your daughter.

As you prepare to relinquish your rights as my mother, as if you were never a mother in the first place, I recognise with gratitude that you have acted from a place of pure unconditional love. So, for that, my dear birth mother, I thank you.

Until we meet in this world or somewhere else in the universe.

With love,

Your daughter x

I will continue to suggest writing things down in subsequent chapters too. It is a therapeutic and empowering action to take. When we tangibly commit words to paper (the old-fashioned way) they seem that much more real. Plus, the page never talks back to you! I have found that writing helps me let go of things that I cannot change and when I have finished I feel relief.

Now go write…

Chapter 3

Truth and Lies

Sometimes We Lie to Ourselves and Others

The half-truth is the most dangerous form of lie because it can be defended in part by incontestable logic. — Manly P, Hall

"Who managed to get paint on the wardrobe door?" My mother screeched at Jason and me. She was seething—I could practically see steam coming out of her nostrils. We had been doing an art project in the front bedroom and I had managed to splatter paint on the antique wardrobe doors. I felt sick to my stomach, knowing that if I owned up I would get a jolly good hiding.

"I don't know how it happened," I lied, hoping she would believe me.

"Well it didn't paint itself Joanna. One of you must have done it, so who was it?" She asked again looking like she might explode any moment.

"It was Jason!" I blurted out, "But it was an accident," I said trying to diffuse the situation. Jason gave me a look that made me feel sick inside. It was a look of horror and betrayal. He was shaking, denying it totally.

"It's wasn't me!" he pleaded, "It wasn't me!"

"Was it you Joanna?" She asked again.

"No," I replied, lying through my teeth.

Mum was satisfied she had the culprit and gave Jason an almighty wallop. He cried pitifully and looked at me as if to say, "How could you?" I felt awful but relieved that it wasn't me getting the wallop. Lying about things I did began to become easier.

****

****

Children who lie are often doing so as a warped substitute for love and affection. I think this was my reason for doing so. I lied because I did not want to be seen as doing wrong. I wanted to be seen as the good girl, the perfect girl, the one who wouldn't be discarded for doing something wrong. It was a moment to deflect the blame away from myself. Many adoptees live in a constant state of anxiety and fear with a primal sense of insecurity. Lying gives you a sense of control because it allows you to manipulate things and people around you. This sense of power can feel like it fills the void that was left when you were separated from your birth mother. Lying in small children is normal though, and in the early stages they cannot tell the difference between truth and fiction. It can be seen as part of the creative process. However, when lying becomes a conscious fabrication of the truth in order to hide something then it can become more problematic. If not dealt with properly in one's childhood years it can often develop further with age. I know that for me lying as a teenager became a way to control my freedom. It was like I was leading a double life.

There is such an uncomfortable internal tension when you act like one person and feel like another. What you believe about yourself is what guides your actions. Adoptees can seldom be wrong in their own minds and will defend their beliefs (however wrong) just to prove a point. Even if those beliefs are based on someone else's interpretation of what you ought to think or do, when you internalize them they become your truths and can restrict you from living your life to the fullest. Let's re-evaluate your truths so that you can become much more authentic and reveal the true you that is bubbling inside, desperate to explode out, the authentic you. Renowned author and researcher Dr. Brené Brown says that "Authenticity is the daily practice of letting go of who we think we are supposed to be and embracing who we actually are." So, stop living how you 'ought to' and start living how you want to.

****

****

I was feeling anxious as I held the envelope from the adoption agency that had long ago placed me with my adoptive parents. I had been searching for my birth mother, and this envelope contained part of my story. There was a moment of hesitation as I asked myself inwardly, "Are you ready to read this?" An overwhelming feeling of trepidation overcame me. I half imaged that I might be opening Pandora's box. Once open, would I be taunted by whatever was released and never be able to contain those things again? I had no idea. I felt like I was about to leap out of a plane at 25,000 feet without a parachute. Terrified, I summoned every ounce of internal courage I could muster. Not wanting to unleash anything uncontained, I opened the envelope carefully, slowly peeling back the flap for fear of ripping the paper inside, this paper containing information that up until this point was a mystery to me. Whilst a part of me desperately wanted to open the envelope, another small part did not. Once the letter was opened and the information consumed, I could never go back. I had the power in my hands to change everything I knew, or thought I knew, about myself. It was a power I was not accustomed to, it scared me witless. I started to pull out the letter inside. It was official, it was real, and it was happening to me at that very moment. It took forever and yet no time at all to release the letter from its protective envelope. I inhaled deeply. This was it. This was my moment to find out about the woman who had carried me for nine months, who chose not to have an abortion and who gave me away. This was the biggest opportunity of my life —the opportunity to find out about my birth mother.

I looked down at the typed letter. The first part was a fairly short account of the kind of girl my mother was: her academic and personal qualities. She was training as a Nursery Nurse in London, was a good student and keeping up with the work set. It told me she was easily led and a bit 'boy mad'. Overall, it seems she was a decent person from a good family with no serious issues. She was not a princess or a famous movie star. She was an ordinary person, but she was also my birth mother, which in itself made her ordinary seem extraordinary. As I read further through the paperwork one word leapt off the page and hit me between the eyes like a cold silver bullet—rape.

My birth mother had been raped and I was the result.

The bullet exploded in my head, my skull pounded with anxiety and I felt sick to my very core. Rape, a filthy, dirty, appalling word that reeks of violence, instantly dispelled the picture I had fabricated about my conception. I had always imagined a passionate affair. The idea of being the offspring of a rapist sent shivers down my spine. Was I tainted in some way? After all, I had my birth father's DNA, so this criminal was a part of me. I felt worthless, unwanted, like I had suddenly lost part of myself. The me before I had learned about my conception was gone. Now lost forever, I felt like she had floated out to sea and drowned. Why, oh why, did I want to know about my birth mother? Had my fears been realized—had I just opened Pandora's box?

I kept reading that sentence in my records over and over again, thinking, hoping that the words would change, or I had read them incorrectly. But they did not change; they remained indelible on the page, becoming imprinted in my mind. I felt rotten to the core—born from violence, not love. I was an accident, not just an accident but a terrible toxic side effect. It was a bitter pill to swallow. I felt like I had been thrown through the windscreen of life and landed in a crumpled heap on the tarmac. Waves of negativity and self-deprecation washed over me, and I just sat with my birth records in my hand trying to make sense of what I had just learned. I wanted to dissolve, to melt away into the background and to just make it all go away. My mind began to create stories. Did she lead him on? Was she being provocative? Did she just say she was raped to get out of a tricky situation, or did she really enjoy it? I imagined the scenario, the story, as if it were a movie. I watched as someone played my birth mother and saw her being raped. The movie reel looped over and over. The sick feeling in my stomach intensified.

A sudden wave of guilt washed over me. What the hell was I thinking? I tried to imagine how my birth mother must have felt, especially carrying me around inside of her for nine months, a constant reminder of a traumatizing experience. Every time I moved inside her, how must she have felt, for every twinge and pang did it take her back to my conception? "Oh God, oh God… help me, please," was all I could think. The tears welled up. I felt ashamed, ashamed for her but also ashamed for me. All my life I had been seeking a connection to my birth mother and the first thing I learned about her is this harrowing experience we both shared. I, too, had been raped. Guilt *set in, guilt for my birth mother having to carry me for nine months and guilt over my own experiences. This realization brought up all my past feelings of having my own first child adopted in a wild tumult of emotion (discussed in more detail in Chapter 7). I cried for him. I cried for me, for my loss. I cried for my rape and the fact that I could not have stopped it. And I cried for my mother. I cried pitifully, endlessly for all the times in the past I had held on to my tears.*

I ran to the mirror to study myself, to see if I could tell what I had inherited from my birth father and what from my mother. I attributed the physical traits I did not like to my birth father, wondering which, if any, of his other traits lurked beneath my surface. Did I have a deviant gene, was there a black streak running through me? I looked and felt like shit, feeling like I had caught a mysterious disease that I would now have to live with for the rest of my life. I had always known I would have been considered 'illegitimate' but now, to add insult to injury, I was the product of a rape. No wonder my birth mother relinquished me for adoption. How could she possibly have kept me? I would have been a constant reminder of an experience she would much rather forget. In that moment, I felt crippled inside, hating myself deeply.

****

****

We are not exact clones of our parents; we are each unique evolutionary beings. Though I grieved for the lost me in that moment, eventually, after many years, I came to the realisation that the story I had been telling myself was utterly untrue. What we believe to be true and what is actually true are very often not the same thing. What we tell ourselves is what we believe, even if it is a lie. I did not have a mysterious disease or inherit some awful trait that would tar me forevermore. Yes, I am the result of rape but that had not defined me as a person before I knew, and I would not allow it to do so thereafter.

We are so trussed up by our belief systems that our version of what is real is just that—*our* version and no one else's. Our own perception of what is true defines our reality; what we believe is what we act on. It took me several years before I could change the story internally. My original conception of it was powerful, dark and foreboding in a way that gripped my mind with such ferocity and made me believe I was unworthy of any love. You, too, may have had experiences prior to your adoption that inform your beliefs, beliefs such as being unlovable, imperfect or even a reject. These are complete falsehoods, lies which you may have even defended as your own pure truths.

When we believe a story with total certainty we live out that story, whether or not it serves us. I once spoke to myself with such hate. I believed my own lies and got sucked even deeper into a spiral of self-loathing. What you focus on is what you feel—the more I focused on self-pity the worse I felt, and the worse I felt the sorrier for myself I became. It is a vicious cycle, a self-fulfilling prophecy.

I pulled myself out of that cycle by reading about others who had been conceived through rape and it became clearer to me that whilst being the product of rape is devastating news it did not mean that I was tainted in any way. The more I read the less guilty I felt. I became more empathetic towards my birth mother and I began to feel an affinity for her and the struggle we had both gone through. I started to believe that the story I had been telling myself was untrue; I was not the clone of a rapist and I was not guilty of anything. Revealing these as lies and focusing on the truth opened me up to such relief.

For many adoptees lies can become easy to believe. If you spend your life making up stories about yourself or your birth family and denying the trauma that you faced as a child, it may protect you in the short term, but it results in you becoming complacent. In the long term this numbing or dumbing down of the reality of your trauma can often lead you to simply accepting it without question. Ignorance is not always bliss, and if you continue to lie about how you feel, chances are you will live a life far less blissful than you deserve.

I once saw myself as the clone of a rapist, a horrid person. This deeply affected my self-image; I was angry inside and I lied to myself because I could not express how I really felt. For some people the effect of lying to yourself can lead to far darker places —addiction, self-destructive behaviours, depression and a myriad of other struggles that can distract us from addressing the root cause of all these symptoms. The sad and often uncomfortable thing about this is that we may know these behaviours are ultimately damaging to us, yet we will continue to embrace them instead of confronting the real underlying issues. We become so attached to our awful predicament that it becomes our norm, comfortable and familiar, even becoming defensive and offended if someone challenges us.

Self-Check-In

Imagine if you could just stop lying to yourself about how you feel, about your birth mother and your adoption. Imagine that you could break out of the hard shell that surrounds you and live a more authentic truthful life. How might that look for you?

I think that for many of us lying means that we do not have to take responsibility for or face the consequences of how we really feel. We allow ourselves to wallow in self-pity and rationalise our behaviour, becoming just another sad story of adoption filled with lies and rejection. What I realise now is that after years of negativity all that I was doing was cutting myself off from a deeper authenticity of self. I am a really great person. You are a really great person. But we have been absolving ourselves of the responsibility for being that person with the lies we have been believing. I have now claimed myself as the great person I know I am and I am very happy with her. I think it would be amazing if you did the same.

****

****

Chapter 3 Personal Alchemy Exercise

There is tremendous personal power to be gained from standing in your own truth and authenticity and the following exercise is one way to help you do that. This is an opportunity to find out what you truly say to yourself when you are on your own, without the mask that you wear for others. These are your underlying truths. They are ingrained in your subconscious mind and form the fundamental cornerstones of your belief systems. This is an exercise in self-reflection.

1. Open to a new page in your journal and draw a line right down the middle of it.

2. In the first column, write down all the things about yourself, others and the world around you that you believe to be true. It may be a long list!

3. Read the list back to yourself. Does it surprise you? Consider where you think those beliefs come from?

4. In the second column identify if those beliefs are really true. Why do you believe they are true? You may find that for some of the things you have written, upon deeper consideration, are actually false. For example, you may write something like, "I doubt that I can be happy." Is this really true? Why? Or have you just accepted this to be true without really asking yourself if it is valid? Dig deep and allow your answers to come from within. Let your intuition guide you. Write down anything that comes to mind even if it makes no sense to you at all.

5. Once you feel you have totally exhausted your list and have determined which are true and which are false, you can start to reframe how you think about them.

6. Replace the false truths with new *real* truths, even if this requires a new page to work on. Write the total opposite by its side. For example, instead of "I doubt that I can be happy," write "I choose to be happy every day."

7. Now look at everything you have written and create a mantra or affirmation to use daily that reinforces your positive truths. For example, "I believe that anything is possible for me; I live authentically and see my own self-worth."

8. If you really struggle to believe what you are writing and find it difficult to use the present tense, I have found it very helpful to write, "I am open to..." happiness, love, success or whatever it may be. You might not be there, but you can always be open to things.

9. The more you repeat your new truths and affirmations the more they will become your beliefs. Do not

concern yourself with how this happens. Just do it and trust that it will work.

Chapter 4

Ditch the Label

You are not just an adoptee

I'm myself, not a label — John Brunner

I was never very gifted at maths, in fact, I truly detested it. I had a kind of maths dyslexia and would get myself tied up in terrible knots trying to work things out. I just could not see how the numbers fit together. I felt an extra pressure in my maths class, because my dad was a teacher and one of his subjects was maths, so I always felt especially hopeless when number work didn't click with me. It wound me up no end. Mr. Jones, the maths teacher (who I really didn't like), called me 'Weary Went' (Went was my adoptive surname). He would say it openly in class, labelling me for my poor grasp of numbers and ridiculing me in front of classmates. He seemed to take an inordinate amount of pleasure from pacing up and down the classroom with a sneer on his face as I remained unable to answer the questions he constantly threw at me. He made me feel humiliated and embarrassed.

My school maths report suggested that, "Joanna has the ability but lacks the concentration." I don't think anyone ever worked out if I had the ability or not. There just seemed to be an unfounded assumption that because my dad was a teacher and one of his subjects was maths I should have inherited his brilliance. Of course, no one considered that I was adopted and thus could not possibly have inherited any of his mathematical competencies! Being labelled as 'weary' in maths stuck with me. My self-image developed around the fact that I was utterly rubbish at maths, which then expanded to everything else as well. So, I lived up to the label and remained totally hopeless at maths throughout my school years and beyond.

"I can't do maths," I would plead with my dad when he tried to get me to do my homework, when he tried to get me to understand how numbers worked and when he got me to go over and over and over formulas to try and help me, which all just led to him getting frustrated with me and me getting frustrated with myself and upset with him. In the end, he gave up and so did I. The label meant that I, and everyone else, had much lower expectations of me and my abilities in maths.

One of my very first labels was on my adoption papers. 'Failure to thrive', meaning that I wasn't putting on the weight they had hoped for a premature baby like me. It was a term used for all babies that were not progressing as they should. Already, someone could be a failure right from birth! As I got older, my mum would often say how very, very stubborn I was. And there was another label for me and again one with derogatory overtones. I did not have much going for me, really. Adopted, 'stubborn', 'weary' and a 'failure' from the start.

One day in the late 70's I visited my dad in the local psychiatric hospital where he'd been admitted for manic depression, I was waiting for him in the art therapy room. An orderly walked in and directed his gaze to me. "It's time for lunch dear," he informed me. I was filled with a sudden dread. Did I look like a loony?

"Oh, I'm—I'm visiting my dad here," I hastily stuttered, praying he believed me. The orderly looked a tad embarrassed, apologised and quickly left. I felt uncomfortable at the possibility of wearing a 'loony' label. I felt that it was *the kind of label that one ought to be ashamed of, as if you didn't quite make the grade and were lacking something that was essential to be a 'normal' person. This was such a superficial thought but, as a teenager, what others thought about me was hugely important.*

The moment the orderly left I felt sick, sick that for a fleeting moment I was seen as someone I was not. It was one of those horrid moments that puts a knot in your stomach as if something terrible is about to happen. I now know that feeling is one of pure panic. My dad often embarrassed me with his manic behaviour and so to be even considered a 'loony', albeit very briefly, made me feel extremely uncomfortable. I certainly didn't see myself fitting that particular label.

Like many adoptees, in my early teen years I started asking more questions about my adoption story. I wanted to know more about my start in life and why I was adopted. I wanted to know what traits I may have inherited from my birth family. My dad told me I was illegitimate. I recounted this to someone in school who said that was the same as being a bastard. It felt hateful. Kids in school used the word bastard when they were being unkind to

each other. I didn't want to be a bastard, so I labelled myself as 'illegitimate'
which felt the lesser of two evils. At that time, I felt horrible. It was a word
that instilled a deep and intense sense of shame in me. I felt that being
'illegitimate' would separate me from my friends and that they might
discriminate against me for my difference, for being a bastard, born out of
wedlock. In order to protect myself and prevent that from happening I
allowed my friendships to be superficial so that when the inevitable happened
it wouldn't hurt so much. It was a practice that I became proficient at for
many years and that played out even in my more intimate relationships. The
mere word 'illegitimate' suggested that I was unlawful by nature, born outside
of the law. This left a deep impression on me, affecting me at multiple stages
of my life. When I later became pregnant in my teens with an 'illegitimate'
child I felt that I had done something terribly wrong and even against the law,
and with that followed a new set of labels that I was ready to hang around
my neck such as 'slut' and 'promiscuous' as well as labels like 'stupid' and
'idiot'. They all seemed to hang quite comfortably. It can feel easy to add a
label, that way you never need to look any deeper.

****

****

Labels can have a profound effect on people in many ways, and adoptees no different. As I got older, I was continually unable to shake off the strongest label of them all, 'adopted'. It caused me to feel insecure and inferior. Often, and especially in the media and film, adoptees are labelled as 'damaged' with a propensity for untoward behaviours, addictions and even suicidal tendencies. We are damaged goods with an inherent and undeniable flaw. That was me, 'damaged' and 'flawed'. I became the epitome of my label and it even became somewhat convenient for me. It was my excuse to play the victim, to feel self-pity and to manipulate others into feeling sorry for me. I'd often use my adoption label as a 'get out of jail free card' when things got tough for me and weren't going my way. "It's because I'm adopted," I'd hear myself say whenever I tried to justify any behaviours or actions that were questionable. It was my way of not taking responsibility for my life. I used it to manipulate others around me, to be in control of events rather than being truly engaged in them. This was my way of working with the labels other people had assigned to me, but in truth it was quite toxic and only caused me to become further entrenched in the very labels I was wielding.

The adoption label is further compounded by the two most frequently used and emotion laden labels 'chosen' and 'special', which may not seem like negative labels on the surface but can have a host of effects on those assigned them. Are you an adoptee that was told you were either of these things? For some of you the fact you were 'chosen' or 'special' may give you a feeling of self-worth. However, for many adoptees (myself included) these labels can translate into adoptees conforming to what their parents and others want. The very idea of being 'special' or 'chosen' means that you have to do more than others in order to live up to those expectations, or at least that is what I believed. These two labels can also lead to adoptees becoming very self-obsessed. How can you tell if you are self-obsessed? Ask yourself how often you check the number of 'likes' you get on

Facebook! Another indicator is how you talk about your birth mother. Do you constantly judge her for giving you up, leaving you, rejecting you no matter the circumstances of your particular adoption story? Given the many stresses that stem from adoption it is understandable that you may feel this way, but the added pressure of labels like 'special' or 'chosen' can exacerbate these issues.

Sometimes when I wanted to feel okay about my adoption I would hang on to the 'special' label as it made me feel that there must have been something good in me to make my parents adopt me. But other times, when I thought about being 'chosen', I would get to thinking about what the criteria was for choosing me. Is it like choosing a new puppy or kitchen appliance? How is the choice made? Did your parents get sent lots of photos of cute babies and kids and then just pick one? What was it about you that meant getting chosen whereas other children just got rejected? For so many adoptees, and perhaps you too, the very thought of being a 'chosen' child leaves a sour taste in the mouth.

To be 'chosen' surely means one must have been 'unchosen' at some other point. The myriad of labels that stem from being adopted vary for each individual, but the fact of the matter is that these labels, whatever they may be, can be hurtful, manipulative and wholly damaging to one's general wellbeing.

Try to consider the labels that we use daily without even thinking about it; we define and categorise people into neat little boxes without any conscious thought. These labels conjure up specific reactions in us and others, which at times can be hurtful and judgmental. It is easy to stand on the sidelines and judge others without any deep knowledge or consideration. The names and labels that we attach to ourselves and others do not always accurately portray the person in question. Rather, they are limited assumptions based on our beliefs and opinions without much regard for what we are actually labelling.

Of course, there are so many different sections of society to differentiate that labelling has become part and parcel of what people do. We compartmentalise others, fitting them into neat stackable boxes. The thing is, labels are just words. They are not the person; they just describe the person. Labels are what happen when you make a face-value judgement about someone without actually finding anything else out about them. Maybe we feel safer this way. But it creates a terribly skewed perspective on someone, not only is it skewed but it can also be dangerous. When we compartmentalise someone we lose the opportunity for a deeper connection with them, even with ourselves. The true self fades into insignificance behind its labels and becomes just another cog in the machine. It is dehumanising. It can be easy to believe that the person is their label. Though they are, of course, not. Labels can be divisive, but you are far more than just a label.

> ## Self-Check-In
>
> Are you stuck in your story? Does the label of adoption inform you of who you really are? Are you using the label of adoption to your own advantage in some ways? I really do not mean to sound accusatory here. Believe me, I used the label of adoption to my own advantage for years. But it is one of those hard questions you must ask yourself, and when I asked myself, I heard a resounding "yes," back.

I was even using the label of adoption to remain stuck in my story. It can feel quite convenient and safe because it is always nice to know that there are a bunch of other adoptees all stuck in their stories too. You can identify with them, their trials and traumas and it makes you feel all warm and glowy, less isolated. Do you use Facebook, Pinterest or any other form of social media? Look up adoption. There are hundreds of groups where adoptees can rant, scream and wallow in self-pity and thus have their feelings validated and normalised by other adoptees. This can help you accept what you are going through and give you a sense of solidarity with others. There is a glaring problem with this coping mechanism though. If you label yourself as adopted from a derogatory perspective you can end up stuck in a little adoption box with a very narrow perspective of the world. It is almost like a self-imposed exile from the rest of the human race. It is a very disempowering position to be in, one that eats away at your self-worth. The net effect being that you slip into the easy way of denying any responsibility for your own behaviour using the adoption label as an excuse. I did exactly that, time and time again, but I understand why now. It was the need to give myself an identity.

I wore the adoption label for half my life. It was such a large label that it obscured me from view. This label not only obscured me, but it also set me apart from nearly everyone else I knew. Behind the label was a child, a girl and eventually a woman desperately seeking to be seen. Does that sound a bit like you? Do you, too, desperately want to be seen as something other than someone 'adopted'? You are not defined by your adoption. You are not adoption. You are *you*. It can be challenging to let go of the labels we attach to ourselves as it is convenient to fit into a clearly defined role. But we are not one thing, not one label, and to ditch the labels we attach to ourselves can lead to a dramatic sense of freedom.

****

****

"What would you say if I changed my surname to Patience?" I asked my birth aunt.

"I'd say it was the next logical step for you," she replied, as if it was the most natural conversation in the world to be having. My heart raced, my insides did tumbles, and I felt an excitement rising in me. I had to phone Buntie!

"Hello, it's Jo. I was wondering, what you would think if I changed my surname to my birth name?" I blurted it out on the phone before I could even think of how best to ask her. I needn't have worried.

"Oh Jo, I think that's wonderful," she said with such enthusiasm that I immediately knew it was the right decision. That was it, I would change my name by deed poll and reclaim my birth surname. Changing my name would be a powerful statement. I needed to dig deep and see who I really was inside. I wanted my name to reflect the person I was becoming and not the scared child that had ruled my life for so long. I wanted it to feel right. I wanted to feel that the name I picked would reflect the person I have now become as a result of everything that had gone before. It made sense to me. It sounded right and the more I said my whole new name, JoJo Miracle Patience, the more I felt it was a true reflection of me (we will discuss the importance of miracles more in Chapter 8). So, I took a leap of faith and did it! I changed my name by deed poll, and as soon as I did I felt amazing!

****

****

Your name is your contract with the world. It is the first label anyone will know you by and your membership into the club of human beings. It separates you from others and gives you an identity. But often adoptees do not feel that their name really is their true identity. It was the identity society forced on us and as far as I was concerned it just didn't fit me anymore. I'd grown out of it. My life had always felt like a bit of a jigsaw puzzle that I could never quite find the last few pieces of, one of those 2500-piece jigsaws where you lay it out on the dining table and put one piece in place every time you walk past it. You know you are three quarters through the puzzle and you can see the picture clearly, but you just cannot find the right piece of blue sky you need. In fact, all that is left of the puzzle is the blue sky. It is wildly frustrating, but you want to complete it for your own personal challenge. Changing my name was like finding the key piece I needed to make the rest of the puzzle fall into place.

If I told you that changing my name gave me an entirely new lease on life, it would not be an exaggeration in the slightest. It's not that I need outside influences to feel happy. Personally, I believe that happiness is an inside job and resides in us from birth; it just gets knocked out of us as we grow up. I certainly feel happier now. In a way I have been reborn so part of me now is once again that new baby born with inherent happiness. Yet I still maintain my strength and maturity as an adult and can defend myself against anyone who would try to bring me down. The opportunity to be reborn during my own lifetime, now that is one amazing miracle.

Changing my name was my way of acknowledging my rejection of all other labels that had been assigned to me throughout my life. There is a real opportunity for you to do the same by rethinking your labels and turning negatives into positives. Imagine if my mother had used the term 'free spirited' instead of 'stubborn'? How much more creative it would have made me seem. Though the behaviours I displayed that caused the 'stubborn' label wouldn't change, 'free spirited' feels much more positive and reactions to the label *would* change. My mother, rather than getting bloody annoyed with me, might have seen me in a different light and therefore treated me differently. I would have felt more empowered, and our relationship could have been better, coming from a place of love and not fear.

Labels, the adoption label in particular, are things that we use to classify ourselves. That feisty ego I mentioned before creates a persona based on the things we tell ourselves as well as the things that others tell us. Chances are the things you tell yourself are not always very nice. Negative self-talk can have dire consequences on your physical, mental and spiritual health. It is just so undermining to your being and it can exaggerate every little niggle you feel. You become what you think you are and your behaviour validates it.

I had to do a lot of inner work on self-love before I felt able to shrug off my adoption label. But it is not insurmountable. Once you understand that your adoption label is really quite limiting, keeping you firmly within a little box with no room for movement, then you can start to untie the cord that it has formed around your neck and let the label fall to the ground. So how can you free yourself and untie the adoption label from around your neck? Firstly, you really have to ask yourself a big question. Yes, I know I've suggested you ask yourself a lot of questions over the last several chapters, but they need to be asked. So, ask yourself. Am I happy to be the person I am right now? By asking that of yourself really you are asking if you are happy to be defined by your adoption label. You cannot change the fact that you are adopted, however, you can change the way you think about it and identify with it. You may feel that you can't change the way you think about it. And if you can relate to that, then I challenge you to just say something positive about yourself out loud right now. The ego loves to bring you down, so it can do its job of protecting you. Challenge it by just saying something positive about yourself right now. Labels may derive from outside sources, but the way you internalize them and react to them are completely under your control.

****

****

Chapter 4 Personal Alchemy Exercise One

Sometimes it's the simplest of things that have the most profound effect. This simple exercise is designed to help you shift your mindset when you get totally stuck with your adoption label.

- Sit in a quiet place where you'll be undisturbed for a few minutes, get comfortable and gently close your eyes.

- Imagine that one of your negative labels is written on your forehead with a white board marker (the type of marker that is easily rubbed off).

- Imagine you are using one finger to rub off the negative words.Then write something positive in their place. Words are very powerful, and if you choose wisely you can become what you think.

    For example, if you feel that you don't deserve love, imagine those words on your forehead, and then get your finger and just swipe them off! They rub off really easily.

- Now imagine writing "I am worthy of love," instead This time imagine it's in permanent marker, so you can't just erase it with a finger swipe.

This might seem like a ridiculously silly exercise to you, but I can tell you that small things like this can have a big impact. The more we tell our subconscious mind the positive stuff, the more we will believe it. You can use any analogy that resonates with you, and you can even make your own up. The essence here is to just do it. Do not to allow the negative labels and beliefs surrounding them to fester forever. Once you start it gets easier to ditch the labels you attach to yourself.

Chapter 4 Personal Alchemy Exercise Two

If you are having trouble rethinking your labels in a more positive light and need to first distance yourself from your adoption label, then this exercise will help you do that.

- Take your label and send it on a rocket ship out into space. Imagine that the rocket is zooming at warp speed out into a limitless ether. It goes beyond our current universe and all other universes. It is on a one-way trajectory, and there is absolutely no way it can change course. If by some chance the label does return, just stick it back in the rocket and send it off again, really see it disappearing into space.

Feel this, believe it and take charge of it. Figuratively, in your mind, (or even physically if you prefer) stick two fingers up and just say, "Fuck off, I don't need you."

Chapter 5

The Biggest Decision

Search and Reunion

It is in your moments of decision that your destiny is shaped.

— Tony Robbins

"Why do you want to find your birth mother?" asked my therapist.

I knew this question was coming and yet I did not have a clear answer for her right away. After some time, I responded.

"I just want her to know that I am not angry with her and that I forgive her for giving me away." I hoped that was reason enough for the social worker to arrange a meeting with her once I had managed to track her down. I wanted to see the woman that had given me life, to hear her voice and to feel her touch. I wondered if I might recognise her voice if she had talked to me whilst she carried me. I wanted to look into her face and see something I

recognised. I wanted to be her baby. I desperately wanted to curl up in her arms and for her to tell me she loved me always.

"You'll have to find out as much information as you can about your birth mother's whereabouts and then come back to us."

It seemed like an insurmountable task. I'd have to trawl through hundreds of birth, marriage and death records in London armed with just my birth name and my birth mother's name. I felt overwhelmed. I could not do this on my own. I did not know how to respond or react. I needed a good friend, and luckily, I had an amazing friend. In fact, he was the minister of our local church and had become a trusted family friend to my husband and me. Our children loved him, and he had an innate wisdom that meant he would always have an answer for any question.

"Dan," I asked him, "would you mind coming to London with me to help me search for my birth mother?"

"I'd be delighted," he replied with excitement. And so, the next phase had begun, the search for a fairy tale ending.

The idea of flicking through page after page of records in huge books was not a task that I relished. So, in true JoJo style, I broke open a small bottle of brandy to ease the stress of it. However, I needn't have worried. Within half an hour of searching Dan came to me and said, "I think I've found her!"

My heart leapt, and I felt it pounding in my chest as if it wanted to rush out of my body to the record itself and take a look even before I myself got there. It was true—Dan had found the record. It showed my birth mother's name and her marriage details plus where she had lived prior to being wed. The likelihood of her actually still living there was remote, but it was a clear lead that I could take back to the social worker. I was excited and nervous at the same time, so I nipped out for another cheeky swig of brandy!

From there followed a series of electoral roll searches and eventually I was able to go back to the social worker with the last known address of my maternal grandmother. "I will write a fairly innocuous letter to your *grandmother and see what happens," the social worker told me, making it sound all rather matter of fact. The letter said that the social worker was trying to trace a woman called Edna about a personal issue that had taken place 32 years previously and that if the occupier of the house knew her would they kindly pass on the letter. Less than a week after the letter had been posted my social worker telephoned me.*

"Jo, your birth mother has rung me and would love to meet you..." her voice faded into the background. I could not hear what else she said. My birth mother would love to meet me... She would love to meet me. I gasped for breath, feeling like I was choking. This is what I had always wanted, what I'd dreamed of, what I'd hoped would be the light the end of the tunnel. Yet I felt an overwhelming sense of panic and dread. What if she doesn't like me? What if she is desperately disappointed in me? What if...

****

****

Searching for your birth mother can be one of the most challenging and comprehensive activities that you can undertake. It can be exhausting, both emotionally and physically. The need to search is so unrelenting that for some adoptees it becomes all-consuming. Some seem to be completely ambivalent towards searching. Whilst others may not have the ability to search because they have no access to their records. For those that do search we each have our own reasons and yours may be different from mine. For many, there is a conflict between seeking one's birth mother and not wanting to upset their adoptive parents. I did not struggle with that as I just decided not to tell my adoptive parents. Some might consider that wrong, but it was the right choice for me. Not all adoptees want to search for their birth mother, and that's absolutely OK too. You need to do what is right for you and not what others think you should do. I think for many adoptees, and certainly for myself, there is an overwhelming need to feel your birth mother in the flesh. To make real this person who, often, is just an abstract concept. Do you imagine her in all sorts of scenarios? Before I accessed my records, I made up so many stories about the woman she was. I created my own fairy tale.

How has your adoption been? Has it been a happy family environment or one where you have felt vulnerable and alone? There are so many permutations and I do not pretend to have all the answers for every unique adoption story. What I do know is that I was relinquished as a baby, and my adoptive parents did the best they could in spite of my lingering adoption trauma, but now I have found a way to change how I feel and create the life that I really want. Whether or not you had a happy placement with an adoptive family does not determine how you can move forward with your life. You always have a choice. You can choose to wonder about your birth mother or you can seek her out. Admittedly, this is much easier in the UK than in the USA where some adoptee files are kept hidden, and in some cases adoptee records are even altered to suit the adoptive parents. This makes it harder for those that want to search.

Sometimes adoptees start their search only to stop before they get too far. One of the most overwhelming reasons for that is the potential for secondary rejection, which we discussed at length in Chapter 2. However, the more pragmatic reason for searching, or at least having access to your birth records, is the need to find out about your biological family's medical history. It is infuriating and at times even soul destroying to be asked for your family medical history and all you can answer is, "Sorry I have no idea. I'm adopted." As a parent, I wanted to know what traits and potential diseases I might have been passing on to my children. Was there a history of Alzheimer's or cancer? Whatever your reason for searching, there will be at some deep level a real need to connect to your birth mother. Whatever reason you tell yourself, even if you say you just want information about your family medical history, at an unconscious level you will be wanting to close that gaping primal wound. You will want to see yourself in another person. It will be the first time in your life that you recognise where you come from, who you take after and why it is you always play with your left ear when nervous!

There is often so much secrecy surrounding adoption. It can be such a cloak and dagger affair. The secrecy of who your birth family are and the reason why you were adopted could just be the beginning. For so many adoptees this secrecy was intentional as a way of wiping the slate clean so that a baby or small child could be passed off as the adoptive parents 'real' child. However, as you probably know by now, there is no such thing in adoption as a clean slate. You were adopted with a history, a genetic imprint and a deep biological connection to your birth mother. The inherent desire to find your birth mother should really come as no surprise to people. Yet in so many cases it seems like a total shock.

"How come you want to find your birth mother?" people ask. "Your adoptive parents have given you everything you need." That may well be true from a very shallow perspective. But what many adoptive parents in the past, and maybe even still some today, do not realise or understand is that the need to search is driven by a deep yearning to discover who you really are.

****

****

The date was fixed. Our reunion would take place in my social worker's office. I spent the next few weeks playing out different scenarios of how the meeting would go. For my whole life prior to this moment I had cobbled together stories of what I imagined my birth mother to be like. She had been a princess, an actress, was at one point very rich and at another very poor. Every conceivable possibility had been played out in my head. How tall she was, her eye and hair colour, her body shape, her accent, what she ate and how she laughed. I wondered if she felt any of the same anxiety I did and, if so, how she coped.

"What if she really doesn't like me," I asked a friend.

"How could she not?" was their reply.

I sat waiting in the social worker's office. My stomach was full of butterflies flying about in all directions. For what seemed like an eternity I sat and waited. I felt like was waiting outside the maternity unit for new life to arrive, except that it was my own re-birth I was waiting for. I was terrified.

The door opened, and the social worker walked in with my birth mother. She introduced us, and my heart leapt. It leapt for joy, for love and for recognition. It leapt in remembrance of the time she first held me and the first kiss she gave me. I reached out my hand, "Hi, how are you?" I asked her, just as if we'd not seen each other in a week! The social worker left us. My birth mother and I just stared at each other, a spark of recognition flickering deep within each of us.

"Let's find a pub for lunch," I suggested.

"Great idea Joanna," replied Buntie, my birth mother.

As soon as we'd settled down in the corner of the pub with our drinks we began to share snippets of our lives. I told Buntie about my children and husband. I garbled out facts about my life, trying to make up for lost time. Buntie shared different bits about her life too, her two other children and her work; in no time, we were heading back to the social worker's office arm in arm. Our time together flew past and soon I was back home with my husband recounting the day's adventure to him.

It seemed surreal and almost superficial. There were no tears of joy, no roller coaster of emotion. I think that we had both acutely managed our feelings. There were so many questions I wanted to ask, and yet it just didn't feel right to ask them. I wanted to delve more deeply into my conception and to ask how Buntie felt about it. But I just couldn't rake it up for her. She seemed sensitive, vulnerable and reminded myself of me! Wow—she reminded me of me. Of course, she did! This was the first time in my entire life that I looked anyone right in the eye and saw myself. It was like looking in a mirror for the first time (more about this in Chapter 6). It's hard to actually put into words what that felt like. It was like a divine revelation had descended on me as I looked at my mother. Something deep inside recognised her—I'm sure of it—I felt it in my very being.

I had found my birth mother; we were reunited. I should have been dancing on the ceiling in joy, screaming from the rooftops, "Fuck yeah I found her!" Yet I just felt like someone had taken a well packed suitcase and tipped it out into a massive unfolded pile on the floor, messing up the tidiness that had been carefully packed away for years. I couldn't sleep, my head was all over the place. However, something stirred in my heart over-riding the negativity and shaking me to my very core. It was love. I was feeling love for her. The love that only a child can feel for their mother. I gasped, unable to breath. I wanted to scream, to cry, to hug her and to be a baby once more. My heart felt like it was cracking open.

****

****

Searching is not for those with a nervous disposition! I do not say that lightly as searching really is a challenging thing to do on every level. Like me, you may have ingrained negative self-talk built up over years and years. The small child inside of you may resurface and cry out for their mother's love or the need to feel her arms in a mother's protective embrace. Furthermore, you may have your own ideas about what your birth mother is like. You form your thoughts and beliefs through your own filters and perceptions of reality. You may have lived in total discomfort for years not really feeling like you belong, and this often manifests itself in your behaviour towards others. I was often indifferent and cool towards people though I never really meant to be. My ego was protecting me from further hurt, rejection and abandonment. There is no rational logic. These are deeply ingrained behaviours that, if you allow them to, can totally control you. They did me. And all of these issues rise to the surface when you begin your search.

Though I have said that I did not care that I was going behind my adopted parents' backs to search for her, I did feel some occasional pangs of guilt. You might feel that, too, if not sharing your search is the right choice for you. I may have had a dysfunctional upbringing, but it shaped me into the person that I am now, and I know my adoptive parents loved me in their own way. There is a uniqueness about each relationship with adoptive parents and no adoptee will feel the same way when it comes to sharing their search. Going behind my parents back was really the only way I could search as I didn't have the emotional fortitude to sit down with them and explain myself.

Despite all of that, I understood that seeking out my birth mother was the right decision for me and that the results would be more than worth the minor guilt. In order to shape your future, you must be the best version of yourself and (if you have the ability and inclination to do so) searching for your birth mother may help you get there. You have to look at your past not from a place of torment and insecurity but from a more pragmatic angle. You will need to dig deep, look at the limiting beliefs you have and ask yourself if they are really true.

Those types of beliefs are common to many adoptees, including me. Like me, you may search out information and situations to support those beliefs. You may experience incredibly strong emotional responses to all manner of situations, often even overreacting. I have heard adoptees say they wish they had never been born or that they blame their adoptive parents for 'stealing' them from their birth mother. Some adoptees are full of angst and hate and others have deeply ingrained negative beliefs as I did such as: I'm unlovable, I'm not worthy, I don't belong, I have to please everyone, people who love me will leave me and the list goes on.

Self-Check-In

Consider all these beliefs you have about yourself. Try to see past your angst, hatred and ask yourself, are these beliefs really true? You may find that if you actually allow yourself the time and emotional space to consider these beliefs, rather than simply accepting them as facts, that you find they aren't true at all. To revisit this in more detail, see again the Chapter 3 Personal Alchemy Exercise.

Your current beliefs, feelings and behaviours are influenced by what's gone on before, even if they seem totally unrelated. Our futures are inextricably linked to our past, and we must become more aware of how the past affects us to move ourselves forward. Adoptees often develop a sense of insecurity but can't really work out why. You may even suppress your feelings for many years, which is normal for anybody not just adoptees. You have had thousands of experiences as a child and these have all affected your beliefs and behaviours now. That is mind blowing! Initiating your search can be a tangible way to enter your past and face these feelings head on, which will ultimately lead to a much freer future.

****

****

Chapter 5 Personal Alchemy Exercise One

What if after all the anxiety of searching and the feelings of expectation, your birth mother just does not want to know you?

You really have to ask yourself some hard questions before even considering active searching. It is not to be undertaken lightly; like preparing to climb a mountain you need to be fully prepared for every eventuality.

If you are considering undertaking a search of your own, ask yourself:

- Why do you want to search?
- Are you searching to find out more about your birth mother or more about you?
- Are you ready to take what comes with this, whether it's your birth mother welcoming you with open arms or closing the door in your face?
- Do you have people to support you?
- Do you already hate her, or can you search with an open heart and mind?
- Are you ready to confront whatever comes up for you?

If you know the answers to these questions and still feel that you are ready to search, then go for it. It is likely to be life changing.

Chapter 5 Personal Alchemy Exercise Two

I will now share a technique that I have found really helpful when something triggers me regarding my adoption. This can be helpful at any point in one's life but is particularly useful when going through the stress of searching out a birth mother. You might find it helpful too.

Tell yourself that the past is the past and now is now and let yourself really believe it. That might seem blindingly obvious, but in reality, you may still be living in the past without consciously realizing it. Think about it. Do you spend more time focusing on your adoption journey to date or more time living in the fullness of the current moment? Be honest with yourself. For many adoptees, myself included, I spent an inordinate amount of time regurgitating stuff from the past. However, as soon as I recognised that the past has gone, it no longer felt so tangible; I knew that I could not just pick it up and change it. In that recognition, the hold the past had on my present seemed to diminish somewhat, and I could focus more on the current moment and therefore on the future as well. If you find it hard (and chances are you will) to focus on the now and not the past, try this technique. It is called 5-4-3-2-1 grounding and it is brilliant.

Find a quiet space and sit comfortably. Take five deep breaths in and out through your nose.

5. LOOK: Look around you for five things that you can see and say them aloud.

For example, "I see the chair," "I see the table," or "I see the door."

4. FEEL: Pay attention to your body and think of four things you can feel and say them aloud.

For example, "I feel my bum on the chair," "I feel the breeze on my face," or "I feel the material of my dress/trousers against my skin."

3. LISTEN: Listen for three sounds and say them aloud.

For example, "I hear the sound of birds outside," "I hear the sound cars," or "I hear the sound of a cat purring."

2. SMELL: Say aloud two things you can smell.

For example, "I smell coffee," "I smell mown grass," or "I smell perfume." If you cannot actually smell anything then try to remember your two favourite smells.

1. TASTE: Say aloud one thing you can taste.

For example, "I taste tea," "I taste a biscuit," or "I taste a smoothie." If you cannot taste anything then say your favourite thing to taste.

Now, take a few deep breaths in and out through your nose to finish. Notice how you feel. This grounding exercise is great for any time that you feel a tad stressed or overwhelmed and need to be taken out of that state of mind.

Chapter 6

The Jigsaw Puzzle

Where Do You Fit?

The vision that you glorify in your mind, the ideal that you

enthrone in your heart — This you will build your life by,

this you will become. — James Allen

I was rummaging through endless boxes of photographs of my children,

James and Lucy, sifting through photos from across the ages showing the

children from babies to teens.

"What are you going to do with all those?" Lucy asked me.

"I'm making a photo album for Buntie so she can see you growing up," I

explained to her.

It was the least I could do, after all Buntie was their maternal grandmother

and I felt sure that she would appreciate the gesture. I wanted James and

Lucy to feel some kind of connection to their maternal granny to see her as part of their own birth history even though as a child I had not.

Like many adopted children, I had repressed my natural desire to find out where I came from not through any conscious decision simply due to the secrecy surrounding my history. However, within this secrecy my ever-changing ideas about my birth mother naturally developed my curiosity and creativity. I would write stories and plays about abandoned puppies or newborn babies. There would always be a young girl in the stories who would happen across these foundlings in the hedgerows. These stories would rarely have endings, I just could not figure out what the endings might look like. I had no reference point on which to base them, leaving them blank and expecting to fill it in once the ending came to me. But the gaps either remained or were filled in with made up ideas leading nowhere. The characters were all lost, as was I.

Feeling lost as a small child, I would sometimes lie in my bed and imagine who I might really be, attempting to fill in the gaps in my own story that my adoption had left me with. My most romantic notion was that I was the love child of a princess. I imagined what my life might be like, that other me, the *girl who had not been adopted. I would tie myself up in knots thinking about what her life was or would have been like. I felt fear, frustration and foreboding—fear that I might have lost the other me somewhere, frustration that everything I thought I knew was wrong and a foreboding that something dreadful might happen, but I had no idea what. I became increasingly anxious as I approached my teen years. I had questions about my adoption. Why I was given up? Who was my father? Why was I picked by my adoptive parents? But no one seemed to answer. I guess partly because I never asked the questions out loud. I was worried that asking might upset my parents. But I could not help but wonder, who was I?*

My anxiety coincided with the development of asthma, for which I was given the hateful drug Ephedrine. It was like giving amphetamines to a little girl. But I hated that I struggled to breath. My chest would tighten, and I would panic like I was going to die. So, I took the medicine. I developed vivid, terrifying nightmares. For a time, I even had to sleep downstairs with my mum, so she could keep an eye on me. These nightmares were always the same. I would be trapped in a dark maze that never ended, encountering gargoyles, demons, and devil-like creatures that would suddenly appear in front of me causing me to fearfully panic, scream and wake up. My way was always blocked, there was no way around, no way out. I thought it might be the devil coming to get me. I said my prayers to God each night asking him to help me and to ensure that if I died before I woke up he would take my soul. But it seemed He was not on my side; my nightmares continued. Perhaps the devil was trying his luck. A deep angst within me prevailed, along with my lost feelings. I wondered how I fit into everything?

****

****

Have you ever heard someone say that you were 'lucky to be adopted'—lucky to have found a family that wanted you. What an awful comment for someone to make, luck has nothing to do with adoption. I have heard adoptees recount over and over again that people tell them they are lucky and should be grateful. This does not sit well with me at all. The very idea of being taken from your birth mother and placed with unfamiliar people is not lucky at all, far from it. In some cases, it could be the worst possible outcome whilst for others the placement may develop into a loving family unit. However, I am not here to judge the pros and cons of adoption. Regardless of how good or bad your adoption may have been, there is still an assumption that being adopted gives you an identity. It doesn't. There are those that don't see the need for adoptees to find out more about their history. Adoption is seen as a panacea, a child adopted is a simple happily ever after. But that assumption glosses over the most common question amongst adoptees— "Who am I, really?"

The burning desire to answer this question only grows as we continue to age. As a teen, the hormones kick in and the emotions we feel about not knowing are magnified. Sometimes, as a result, teens act out and this was certainly true for me. My mum in particular saw me as an extension of herself and expected me to think and act as she did. But, like many other teens, I wanted to be independent. I wanted to learn more about myself and where I came from. For many adoptees experiencing this, you start to look in the mirror, wondering "Who the hell do I look like?" If you are in a closed adoption, you may have no clue, maybe you have a photo of your birth mother or birth family or maybe you do not. For those in an open adoption, it may be different, depending on the level of contact you get, but still the small nuances of your genetic makeup may elude you.

From 2006 - 2009 I worked on an adoption panel and would get incensed when people commented on the likeness between children and potential adopters. Just because you might look like someone does not mean you suddenly become their flesh and blood. It may help the adopters feel like the child is theirs, as if they birthed them, but for the adoptee it does absolutely nothing to close the gaping hole that is left when they are removed or relinquished from their birth mother. There is an underlying belief in society that a child's identity can easily come from their adoptive parents—that the child would fit nicely into a preformed mould, poured in as a quivering mess and yet turned out neatly formed, holding together well.

A sense of belonging is one of the key fundamental principles that individuals need in order to feel complete, to feel a sense of self. Without it you are in a state of limbo—not quite in your adoptive family and not quite in your birth family—caught between two separate universes. In the film *Sliding Doors*, the central character, Helen, has her life split into two parallel universes based on the different paths her life could take depending on whether or not she catches a tube train. I often felt that being adopted was similar, in that whilst I was in one particular universe, I still wondered what that other universe might have had in store for me. I often felt that there were two Joanna's. One sailed through life doing all the exciting things I had once dreamed of, and the other stumbling along, not resembling anyone around in her family and feeling like God either didn't hear her prayers or was simply ignoring them. You can take a guess which one I was.

Irrespective of how your story manifests in your life, the truth is that we all need to feel like we belong somewhere. You cannot just float between two universes. For many adoptees, there is a pervading sense of not quite being in the right place. Maybe you feel it too. For some, it may feel like you are a spectator in someone else's story. You watch it play out from a distance, unable to do anything about it. You just have to go with it. You would love to change things, but you just can't seem to influence anything. For others, you may feel the need to fight the situations you find yourself in. You become angry and triggered by things such as birthdays and holidays—times that you feel you should be in a different place with your birth family. Like an active volcano, the anger bubbles within and at some point, you will erupt; woe betide anyone caught in the flow. Or maybe you just feel isolated —a lone adoptee with only your thoughts for company. Your ego may attempt to defend you from pain but doing so only exaggerates the effects of your loneliness. You feel hopeless and helpless. You want to know who you look like, where you come from and how the hell to get back there.

I have felt a mix of all those things at various points in my life, but they all centre on the fact that I never felt like I belonged. Feeling like you don't belong and that you don't have your true identity can erode your confidence. It blocks your path, often getting in the way of both your social and professional life. It feels like weeds have tangled up around you and stopped your own roots from growing strong. Without roots we are unstable. Being unstable means, you are repeatedly unable to stand in your own power and unable to exude the confidence to scream to anyone that cares to listen: "I am me, and I am amazing!"

When I met my birth mother it was the first time in my entire life that I looked at anyone and saw myself. It was like looking in a mirror for the first time. It is hard to actually put into words what that felt like, as though a divine revelation had descended on me as I looked at my mother. Something deep inside of me recognised her; I felt it in the very core of my being. Mirroring is something that non-adoptees take for granted. It's like breathing, you just do it naturally without thinking, the way your family members walk, their mannerisms, traits, physical characteristics and even their interests or talents. Those genetic markers are so often taken for granted, but as an adoptee you miss out on all of them. The basic genetic sensory information you need to help you become your own self is lost to us. Finding my birth mother was the first time I started to feel a sense of identity, like I was closing the gap between my alternative universe and the actuality. It was a breathless moment. I felt like time had stood still just long enough for me to see myself in her.

****

****

Meeting my birth mother made me feel like the gaps in my life were closing at last. And yet, though I felt a great satisfaction that we were now reunited, there was still something deeply ingrained in my psyche that stopped me from being the happiest version of me that I could be. I couldn't put my finger on it, and it started to eat away at me. Negative thoughts crept in and began to dominate my thinking. By all my prior logic I should have been the happiest I had ever been, but somehow, I still felt a deep sadness. The sadness crept in slowly, at first, and then gathering momentum as I let it gain a firm footing, and the negativity really took hold.

I was turning against myself. I started getting drunk every evening after work and smoking weed on top of that. After which I would go to the computer and just write whatever was in my head. I joined an online chat room where people read what I had written, validating my feelings. But what was I feeling? I had closed down emotionally yet again and could not quite put my finger on it. I felt angry with myself, I suppose—angry that I'd had to give my own child up for adoption and angry that it still haunted me. I was angry that I was adopted and angry that I still felt like I was in limbo, letting adoption define me as a person. But most of all I was angry for not being able to deal with how I felt. I just didn't know how to cope so all I could do was write. In those moments, I was so very unkind to myself.

I felt broken. I was afraid of myself—afraid of coming unhinged and being vulnerable. I hated feeling vulnerable. I am typically the one who helps others to cope. I am the go-to person for support, love and care. I am the one who is always smiling, always there and always dependable. But I didn't want to be that person any longer. For once, I wanted to be a baby protected by her mother in the womb, just non-thinking and safe. I wanted to belong to my birth mother. I was sinking into the abyss, the abyss that I had created for myself. I couldn't cope. On the outside, my life seemed fine, a loving wife and mother with a successful job. And I was finally a reunited adoptee. I had everything going for me. However, I still felt a real identity crisis. Deep down, I was disintegrating.

****

****

I still did not feel a compelling sense that I belonged anywhere, and I was selfishly stuck in my ego. Ego is a false persona; it is not the real you. Yes, we develop it ourselves but our experiences, behaviours and beliefs are what structure it, so it can never be truly objective. You tell yourself that you are selfish, manipulative, thoughtless and self-centred, and thus you act accordingly. If you feel unlovable, unworthy, second best, your ego will support you.

Such beliefs about yourself may seem true, but it is because you are looking for ways to validate them. We wallow in self-pity and self-hatred for years. These feelings gained momentum in me and eventually I even thought that divorce would make me happier. I thought that the grass would be so much greener. I half expected that life would suddenly deal me a full house. I tried to find God to see what he had to say about it. He said nothing, as usual.

"Listen, God—you fucker—I'm in a pickle and I need some help." I demanded, expecting an answer instantly. He stayed silent.

What I failed to realise then, when I was demanding of God, is that if I had just stayed in the silence, I might have recognised that it could be a place of healing. Instead my old limiting beliefs reared their ugly head, and once again, I felt unworthy of love, success, happiness and anything else for that matter. But there comes a time that you either have to take control and responsibility for how you feel or stay floating between two universes forever, never really feeling comfortable in either. You have to take a long, hard look deep inside yourself and decide to claim your inherent power.

Adoptees tend to hold on to whatever familial information they can and will unconsciously shape their own identity around that. Even if that identity doesn't fit right. Many adoptive parents (mine included) describe their child as their 'special, chosen child' and even that statement can negatively impact the development of an adoptee's identity. Such early descriptors can marginalize an adoptee's sense of identity prior to their adoption, as though their very being only began after getting adopted. You act out a role in a story that someone else has written the script for. Some people liken it to a witness protection program. Everything about your previous life is wiped and you start anew, a totally different person.

Whilst many adoptees believe finding their birth family will just give them a sense of identity, it doesn't. You belong to neither family. I have heard adoptees say they have no identity, but that in itself can be a liberation. It is up to you to create your own identity. This can be a powerful act of self-determination. Basing your identity on your birth family or adopted family or any other outside influences will give you a shadow of a life. Those are all just stories that you tell yourself. Your identity is not (as some may suggest) based on how the world sees you. Your identity is not your job, social life, political status or adoption. Defining your identity is about your own values, how you treat people and allow them to treat you. Your values are what determine the real you, not the veneer that everyone around you sees. We all judge a book by its cover, but that does not define what is on the inside. Adoptees fit into an identity that often leads people to treat them in a particular way, and because of this you may be overlooking the amazing attributes you have, either focusing solely on the negatives or making yourself into someone you're not. It is often easier to conform to another's ideal of who you are than to step into your own uniqueness. But this undermines your self-worth and causes your identity to become uncertain.

I firmly believe that you can create your own identity, one that is built upon your values and not on false assumptions that limit your true self and potential. I have come to the realisation that the story I was telling myself in my head about having lost my identity was in fact just that—another story, one that I had been telling myself subconsciously for years. However, once I came to this realisation I was able to create my own identity and reclaim my power. If you are grappling with your identity, please know that you have the inner magic to unlock your true uninhibited self.

****

****

Chapter 6 Personal Alchemy Exercise

There is an inner magic inside you which, if tapped into, can expand over into your life as joy, happiness and abundance. You can be the person you really want to be. The following exercise is one of self-actualisation, meaning it is an opportunity for self-discovery and growth. It will help you expand your thoughts and clarify your thinking so that you can really start to determine your own identity.

Ask yourself, "Does who you are now limit who you could really be?" Chances are you'll answer yes, because that's what adoptees do. We limit ourselves and stifle the development of our true selves.

- Remember that you are not your thoughts (see Chapter 1).

- Take some time to reflect on the good things that are deep inside you.

- Notice small positive details about yourself. For example, your beautiful green eyes or lovely auburn hair.

- Take note of the great things you do during the day, no matter how small. It may be something good you did at work, like getting something done on time or writing a great report. It might be how your values manifest in each action you take daily. Whatever they are make a mental note, write it down in your journal or keep them typed up in your phone.

- Do not be a slave to your adoption story. Tear down the walls of conformity and the stereotypical adoptee, you know very well the stereotypical actions and behaviours of an adoptee, especially the negative ones. So, when faced with a challenge contradict your usual response by doing something different and more loving to yourself.

- Revisit the truths you identified in Chapter 3. Why do you believe the things you do?

- Expand your thinking. Write down five things that you really want in your life. It might be a work goal or a life goal, such as to travel more or take up a new hobby. For each goal, write in detail what they look like, how you will feel when you accomplish them and how you will recognise when you are where you want to be. Now shut your eyes and visualise each of them as if they have already happened. See how that feels for you. Do not to limit yourself.

Now that you have spent some time clarifying your thoughts in this moments below are five daily principles that I have used to help create my own identity.

- Set an intention for your day or activity that will help you take steps towards what you really want in life.

- List five things you are grateful for at the end of each day.

- Acknowledge but brush aside distractions that stop you from going forward.

- Believe in yourself.

You are actually far greater than you could ever imagine. There is so much potential in you that you would have to live a million or more life times to ever reach it. Learn to dream big for yourself and then dream bigger; surrender to what life brings you and will become the person you truly want to be.

Chapter 7

Open Heart Surgery

No Blood Loss Necessary

Getting over a painful experience is much like crossing monkey bars. You have to let go at some point in order to move forward. — C.S. Lewis

It felt like I was sitting on barbed wire, a punishment for my misbehaviour, maybe they'd stitched me right up and I'd never have sex again, maybe they all hate me. My head was filled with stories. I had to tell myself something to reinforce my feelings of total worthlessness, guilt and shame. I looked around the ward. There were smiling faces, babies crying, people cooing and families celebrating. Then there was me. I wanted to cry, but I couldn't. It was as if I was in an invisible bubble that had accidentally rolled onto the ward. I should have been in another room. The one where they put naughty girls who dropped their knickers.

"I want to see my baby," I said to the nurse.

She looked alarmed, "That's really not a good idea Joanna."

"I really want to see my baby," I implored.

"We are worried that if you see your baby, you will bond, and it will be more difficult to give him away." Give him away. Give him away! That's the phrase she used, like I was giving away a second-hand book. 'Give him away' implied that I didn't care. It suggested I couldn't be bothered with him anymore. I felt anger bubbling. Distressed, my breasts were filling with milk and my hormones racing. I wanted to scream, to plead, to demand, and more than anything I wanted to be anywhere but where I was.

"I have to do this, I won't change my mind I promise, I just want him to know I cared," I begged the nurse.

"Come with me and you can see the baby." She relented. In the nursery, the nurse pointed to a still blue bundle. "This is your baby." My heart leapt. I

wanted to cry, but I wouldn't cry. I didn't want them to think I was weak and helpless. The nurse scooped the little bundle into her arms and held him close to her. He wailed and wriggled. He knew. I knew that he knew: the nurse was not his mother.

"I'm here, I'm here," I tried to telepathically communicate with him. "I love you. Please don't hate me."

There is no greater love than that of a mother for her child. In that moment, I knew that one look was never going to be enough. I had to hold him. There was a deep desire that I'd never experienced before. It was so consuming that I found it hard to focus on anything except the blue bundle in the nursery. Amazingly, the universe answered, and I found myself in the back of an ambulance with three other mothers being taken to a nursing home. I looked down as I cradled my infant son for the first time ever. I peered at his dark blue eyes, his tiny fingers and toes. His perfect nose and lips. He was the most beautiful thing I had ever seen up to that point in my whole life. My heart felt like it would burst wide open, right there in the back of an ambulance. I was overcome with adoration, a feeling so profound that my body tingled, and

I became light headed. It was love. I was feeling love. I don't think I had ever felt anything so beautiful before. I was enraptured. The ten days I spent with my baby seemed the longest ten days of my life. For that ten days, I was his mother—a young, inexperienced, short-term one, but a mother, nonetheless.

A few days later, my parents came to collect me to take me home. I don't even recall saying goodbye. I cried. I didn't stop crying for days and days. I sank into a depression, and I stayed in my room existing on antidepressants, sleeping pills and self-devaluing thoughts. I hated myself. I hated my parents. I hated everyone. I couldn't cope. I didn't know how to cope, I didn't know how to feel other than worthless. I was fragile, broken to pieces and alone.

Eventually, I finally ventured out to register the birth and then, six weeks later, sign the adoption papers. I looked into every pram I passed, expecting and hoping to see my baby boy. I wanted to take the babies I saw. If a baby cried, my heart leapt. If a baby cried, my breasts yearned to feed. And then I walked into a small office all alone and signed a piece of paper relinquishing my parental rights. It felt as if I'd performed my own open-heart surgery.

****

****

For many adoptees we are told to forget about the past and move on. The thing is that adoptees are always tied to their past. Just because you are adopted doesn't negate the fact that you had a birth mother and possibly other family too. Do you find yourself constantly trying to reconcile your past with your present? You can bleed to death emotionally if you do this and it affects everyone around you. I realise now that you don't have to emotionally bleed to death over your adoption. However, what usually happens (and believe me I know) is that we look for reconciliation in all the wrong places. You may feel desperately guilty and angry about your adoption and believe that reconciling your past is the way to healing. The trouble with that belief is that the past is in the past, and no matter how you try to harmonise your past and present, it just doesn't seem to solve the problem. You are probably desperate for reconciliation, and your heart feels like it is breaking, but the more you try to reconcile your adoption journey, the more you sink into the pain you feel. The need for reconciliation can eat away at you, and you can become so obsessed with it that your whole life is governed by that need.

For years after relinquishing my baby, I tried to reconcile giving him up with the opportunities that he would then have as a result. It tore me to shreds. I didn't reconcile anything—it just made me feel ten times worse. I just ignored it and, of course, it festered away, consuming me and affecting my relationships. But you don't have to let it consume you. It's not about forgetting the past like it never happened (because, obviously, it did). It's more about recognising that the past doesn't have to play a role in the now. So many people try to build a bridge between the two, but all that happens is that they travel back and forth over the bridge and, more often than not, have a preferred side. For some it's the past, whilst for others it's the present. That was me, traipsing over the bridge and spending far too much time on the wrong end of it, stuck in the past.

Some adoptees believe that you will spend your whole life reconciling your past with your present, making the case that you cannot disconnect the two. However, I believe that, whilst adoption is a continual journey, there are ways in which you can reconcile the past so that it doesn't continually consume you. You do not have to emotionally bleed to death. The adoptee who spends more time on the far end of the bridge (the past) is more likely to be the adoptee that feels angry, scared, depressed, annoyed and out of sorts. But that does not have to be the case. Do you feel stuck in a rut, like you can't seem to shake it off or are you an adoptee that is creating something amazing for your life right now? You are not an effect of the past. You are not powerless to change how you feel in the present. You can create something amazing for your life.

****

****

"Hello Joanna, it's your uncle Steuart here." I was worried, my Uncle Steuart had never called me before. Something terrible must have happened. My heart started racing. He went on, "I have a letter here addressed to you from a girl who thinks you might be her boyfriend's real mother." I was stunned. "Joanna" —he shook me out of my daydream— "Joanna does this mean anything to you?"

"Ah right, yes I do know what that means. Just pop it in an envelope and send it to me, thank you." I replied casually as if this is the sort of letter you get daily. I gave my friend Neil's address just to be safe.

I hung up. Immense feelings of utter panic, bewilderment, anxiety and excitement hit me all at once. I felt like a headless chicken. My body just moving on auto pilot whist my head was totally disconnected. I could hardly breath; I felt dizzy and hot, and my heart was pounding in my chest. "Oh God, oh God, oh God," was all I could say to myself. I repeated it out loud as I drove back from a meeting to my office. The remainder of the afternoon was a total blur. I couldn't focus on work. It was like I was trying to stand on shifting sands. Everything was changing dramatically, too fast. It all felt *unreal, wobbly as if my very world was changing underfoot. I couldn't get my balance emotionally, and I couldn't think straight. "Get a grip," I told myself. But I just couldn't.*

My son, the child I had always hoped, prayed and at times pleaded with God for, had finally tracked me down. Maybe God had heard me after all. I now stood on the edge of a precipice. There comes a point in life where you have to take stock of where you are, and I knew that if I took a step blindly I'd be falling into a dark void. I had fantasised about the moment my son would find me, and it was nothing like I imagined. I was now met with a choice. I could take a leap of faith, forge ahead and step out in front of me embracing whatever was coming my way or I could retreat from the edge and go back on the path that I'd been on for years. It seemed an obvious choice to make.

"The letter has arrived Jo," my friend, Neil, rang to tell me.

My heart took a leap straight to my throat and got wedged there. I couldn't speak. When I eventually composed myself (after what seemed like forever) I raced around to Neil's house. I was shaking. Shaking with fear, trepidation and anxiety tinged with expectation. I held the envelope in my hands and opened it, pulling out the letter that my Uncle had forwarded. I was about to dissolve on the spot. I couldn't muster up the strength to read it.

"Here, let me read it for you Jo," said Neil, taking control. I loved him for that and always will.

My heart felt like it was going to explode as Neil read the letter from a young woman who believed her boyfriend was the baby I'd given up for adoption 24 years earlier. I burst into tears. I felt scared. Scared of what? Scared of my own son? No, I was scared that I wasn't equipped to handle whatever emotions might surface, emotions I'd been suppressing for 24 years. Scared is an understatement. I was actually terrified. My past had catapulted itself into my present reality.

****

****

We can feel so, so heavy at times, which is kind of weird when you consider that we are mainly just empty space! There is not really an awful lot holding us together so why do we feel such weight on us? It seems that negativity and the past emotional baggage we drag around with us has a kind of heft to it. It drags you down and stops you moving forward creatively and allowing yourself to shine. Carrying the adoption burden and punishing yourself for things you cannot change just weighs you down more. The weight of that primal wound can lead to you not being the best version of you that you can be. It can lead to physical symptoms that affects the immune system. For some adoptees, the weight of our past is such a burden that we sometimes use coping mechanisms like smoking, sexual promiscuity, drug use or over/under eating to compensate for the pain. Don't be alarmed if you recognise yourself here. This is not a judgement about your behaviour it's just recognising how some individuals respond to the past.

Thankfully, there are ways to reconcile the past that bring peace and for some their life might actually depend on it. Amazingly, our body and brain are super resilient, and we can move on from the past to a place of comfort in the present. This is what I've done. I don't feel the weight of the past dragging me down. Instead, I feel light and full of unlimited potential. I'd go so far as saying I feel full of joy and happiness, which for me is such a different place from where I have been in the past.

Self-Check-In

So how can you reconcile the past and make peace with it and yourself? You first need to recognise that you don't have the power to change the past. It's not here anymore. It's gone and only your response to it remains.

Look at your adoption journey and instead of allowing anger, guilt, regret or resentment to overwhelm you, take a big deep breath. Interpret your past in a different way and ask yourself how adoption has made you stronger and what life lessons have you learned as a result. When I did this, I thought about being the result of rape. Instead of allowing the feelings of worthlessness to cloud me I saw how the knowledge of that had built my understanding of what it means to be a miracle.

It can also be extremely cathartic to write down how you feel. Research now suggests that writing down how you feel really contributes to your wholeness. You can write a letter to your birth family (like the exercise in Chapter 2), write to people who have died or anyone that you feel has impacted your current beliefs about yourself. Let out all the anger that is bubbling up inside you. No one else will see these words and letters you write so you can write whatever you like. Swear often, if it helps too. I love using the word 'fuck'. It's powerful.

When you're still stuck in your story it can be easy to find yourself saying 'if only'. If only you weren't adopted, if only you hadn't been born, if only you hadn't done something or other, if only... Jim Carrey has said, "If you aren't in the moment, you are either looking forward to uncertainty, or back to pain and regret." Look back at your regrets, the things that you think 'if only' about. Who were you at that time? What choices did you have? What did or didn't you know then? Has it made you a stronger person as a result? You might actually find out that you did okay then, in hindsight. When I look back at my adoption and the tiny baby I was, I had no choice, I didn't know anything, and I managed to survive and grow to become the person I am today. I'm thankful for that.

In your journey towards performing adoption alchemy and getting out of your story, you cannot get lost in the 'if only' scenarios, but it is still crucial to acknowledge your grief. Many adoptees are stuck in *complicated grief*. It's a real condition that means you are stuck in an intense state of mourning. You can't move on from the loss of your birth mother and it affects everything you do. You experience extreme anger over your adoption and avoid anything that reminds you of it, like birthdays or Christmas. Some adoptees feel that life is meaningless and empty. If this is you, then please seek some therapeutic counselling as sometimes you do need to call in the professionals. If you feel bogged down with grief over your adoption, then connect to those feelings. Allow yourself time to cry for your loss, wail and scream if need be, but without attaching to those feelings just allow them to come and go.

As adoptees, we may find ourselves repeating these harmful cycles again and again, never really creating a change for ourselves. Doing the same old thing and expecting different results is like being on the hamster wheel to nowhere. You go around and around and wear yourself out. You have to accept the past for what it was and move forward. Too many adoptees linger in the past, it's a comfort zone for many. I know, I spent years there. Better the devil you know, right? But being stuck can be all consuming. You can't control the past, no matter how hard you try. It's impossible (unless they invent time travel, of course). Stop punishing yourself and others for your past. The problem with this is that we tend to repeat the things that we punish ourselves for. It's a vicious circle. You have to accept things for what they were, no matter how you perceive them. The trick here is to find a peaceful place inside yourself in order to make peace with the past. Easy for me to say right? But the more we can really focus on the present moment, the now, the more the past will fade. It's still there, but it doesn't play a dominant role in your life. George Herbert said that "living well is the best revenge." That is so true. What George was saying is that it doesn't matter what the past was like, what happened and what was done to you. You can choose to say it doesn't matter and not allow it to control you. You can gain your personal power back by choosing to think differently. Seeking revenge, feeling bitter and blaming your birth mother or adoptive family or anyone else that has wronged you only serves to keep you in the ever-escalating cycle of self-destruction. The alternative is seriously worth a try, especially if you want to feel happy with who you are.

****

****

Chapter 7 Personal Alchemy Exercise

Where is your happy place? Don't laugh, this is not just an exercise for angry kids; this is a great strategy for anyone. I would even go a step further and seek your *peaceful* place, the place where you can calm your mind and connect to something bigger than yourself. You do not need to attach a label to that something but if it helps you can. Use the words that resonate with you, that may be God, Buddha, Allah, Mohammed, Universal Spirit, the universe or any words that you can feel deep inside yourself. The specifics do not matter, rather it is the understanding that there is something greater than yourself that matters most here. What I am advocating here is mindfulness and meditation. But remember, every single day is different. Shit happens, and you feel bad, and on other days you may feel amazing. That is just how life is. However, once you learn to calm down your mind and spend more time in your peaceful place, you can live with more integrity and grace.

This may be tricky to start with, if you have never done anything like this before, but I promise it does get easier with practice. And it is so worth it.

1. Find a really comfortable place that is quiet and away from distractions like your mobile phone, the TV, your kids, etc.

2. Start by allowing yourself 2-5 minutes of your time. Set a really quiet soft timer.

3. Sit or lie down and softly close your eyes if you wish. Sitting straight may be better as it allows you to focus on your breath easier, but if that's a step too far then lie down. Eyes can be open or closed. I close mine as it helps me focus on my breathing. If I find myself nodding off, I half open my eyes and try to look towards my forehead where the pineal gland is.

4. Place your hands where they feel most comfortable. I usually just place them in my lap when seated.

5. Just notice your breath and how it enters and leaves your body or how it feels—don't change or force it—just pay

attention to it and marvel at how miraculous that is. You don't need to remind yourself to breathe, yet the body just does it. Wow! Concentrating on your breath is basically what meditation is. That's it! It's no more complicated than that.

6. I guarantee that thoughts will pop into your head randomly. Try not to get carried away with them. You might be thinking, "I can't bloody meditate," "This is too weird for words" or "I need to go shopping." You might not even notice when the first thought comes, but you'll suddenly think "OMG I'm thinking!" Don't worry, don't be hard on yourself, and just refocus on your breath. Every single time a thought pops in and you chase after it, return to the breath. It is actually on the out breath that most people's minds will begin to wander! Think of your thoughts as friends who have popped in to say hi and popped out again. It does take practice, because you have thousands of random thoughts in the mind popping up all the time. But with practice you can control them. Start off

with just a few minutes. The best time for meditation is first thing in the morning before your brain has had time to collect its thoughts. You can build up to half an hour or longer over time.

7. Here's a quick tip, in order to focus on the breath, I count 1-2-3-4-5 on each in breath and 1-2-3-4-5 on each out breath. It helps to stop the other random thoughts from surfacing. Try it for yourself.

8. If you have unexpected feelings come up, don't be alarmed. It happens somethings. I've had tears roll down my face without even knowing why! It's the subconscious mind doing what it does best. Maybe you feel anxious, or sad, anger or frustration. Whatever you feel, just allow it. Try not to add a story to it, to analyse or think about why you feel them. Just allow them with a sense of curiosity, briefly, then return to your breath.

9. Try and meditate daily. It is far better to do this for 10 minutes every day than to try and cram in an hour once a

week. This is a practice in self-discipline apart from anything else.

10. Once you become more proficient and far fewer thoughts pop into your head, you will start to feel that sense of inner peace and calm.

When you have finished, be grateful for the time you spent with yourself and smile (don't worry no-one will see you grinning like a Cheshire cat). The more you practice this, the more you will feel a deeper connection to your true self and the wider universe.

Chapter 8

Humpty Dumpty

Put Yourself Back Together Again

Sometimes when things are falling apart, they may actually be falling into place. — Anonymous

"Neil, I can't cope," I pleaded as he opened the front door. I was at work when I felt like a steam roller hit me. I just got up from my desk and drove straight to Neil's house. He was always so supportive, and as a drug and alcohol counsellor he'd seen it all before when people fell apart. He knew I was starting to feel overwhelmed with my life and marriage, so he just gave me a hug. His hugs were like a bear's. I felt totally safe with him. Even though I didn't really like hugs, I felt I could trust his. We sat and talked for what seemed like forever, and I shared all my anxieties and woes with him. He never told me what to do; he just held the space, so I could rant and let go. I think that without Neil there at that moment, I would have totally flipped out. I made an appointment with the GP.

"It's hardly surprising that you feel overwhelmed," explained my GP, "being adopted, dealing with the loss of your mother, giving up your own baby, being reunited with both and now having to face your son's family at his wedding. Most people would struggle with just one of those issues."

He was right. I had a suitcase full of stuff that I was dragging around with me. It was so heavy that I knew if I didn't let that suitcase go it would kill me. He helpfully prescribed Prozac, some therapy and signed me off work. Part of me felt relief, relief that I could legitimately feel like shit. Another part of me felt like a total failure. I was in my 40's; I should be nailing life not letting it nail me to my own cross.

I stayed on the Prozac and had counselling for a year and a half. I was looking for a panacea to cure me of how I was feeling. My therapist listened to my story, she let me regurgitate it over and over again. She let me share the pain, the frustrations and the anxiety I felt. She let me tell the story I wanted to tell. She let me miss out the bits I couldn't cope with. I was so stuck in my story that I could not see a way out. I'd shared all this previously with God, *yet he hadn't come up with anything useful either. My therapist, however, was kind and I felt safe for 50 minutes a week with her. She helped me recognise that everything I did was because I felt like I 'should' do it. This revelation helped solidify a decision in my mind: I didn't want to be married anymore. If I wasn't married, maybe I would feel different, right? Maybe I could feel free, maybe I could feel happier, stop drinking, have more money, more independence and be the real authentic unafraid me. The more I focused on what I didn't want, the worse I seemed to feel.*

"I'm not sure why I'm so rubbish at relationships," I told a friend once. "I'm slightly masochistic when it comes to relationships."

"But you seem like the perfect couple," my friend replied. "you're always going out and having fun, and you've got two lovely kids. What more do you want?"

It was true. My husband and I did have fun and lots of it. We had great sex. I had a lovely home, good job, nice car, holidays abroad and lots of friends, but I still wasn't really sure what I wanted from life. I did know that

I deeply wanted to be loved yet I rejected that love with all my being. And in that process, I was hurting myself but also allowing myself to be compliant in fulfilling my desire to please someone. Before I was married, it was a tortuous need I had to fill, the need for human contact, the need to feel wanted and significant, however briefly. I stumbled into marriage not really sure of what I was looking for. I was impulsive and worried that no one would want me, so I proposed to my boyfriend of 3 months. We married 9 months later. We were like chalk and cheese. My husband was loving, kind and considerate. I did love him, but I think he loved me more than I could ever love him. It was an inevitable one-way street. I got married for the wrong reasons. I spent over 20 years digging away at the relationship so that it reinforced my whole belief system. A belief system founded on the idea that I was utterly worthless, that I was not worthy of love and that anyone who loved me would, in the end, not want me.

"I can't see me living with you until I'm old," I told my husband. I could see and feel his hurt, but he seemed resigned to the fact. "I expected this might happen but didn't know when."

Many of our friends said they half expected it. That didn't make it any easier. The wheels were set in motion. We divorced. Fait accompli—a self-fulfilling prophecy.

****

****

Do you ever get days when you feel like everything is an uphill struggle and that you're constantly trying to pull things together? On those days the zing in your heart is so faint that you carry on your life half asleep. You know the feeling, where you think to yourself that there must be something better out there, but you have no idea where to look. You look and look but simply cannot find what you are looking for and, in fact, you've actually no idea what you're looking for at all. But it is definitely not where you are, and you are certain of that.

The thing is, if you focus purely on running away from what you don't want, you tend to spend an inordinate amount of time thinking about it! Maybe you don't want to be in your current job, in the relationship you're in, you feel like you have no success or money in life or you might even wish you were never adopted. You focus more and more on what you don't want, and it becomes a millstone around your neck. The noose tightens, and you can't breathe; you become totally disconnected from life. Your joy and passion seem to have vanished, and you just move through life on autopilot.

The more time you spend thinking about the things that cause you anxiety and distress, the more it triggers you to think of other things in the past that have also caused you anxiety and distress. Your emotions are rather like a raging forest fire; they spread quickly and can get out of control easily. You have to be your own firefighter and totally control the fire. There is absolutely no room for fear because fear will own you and take over. It will stop you dead in your tracks, and you'll choke to death. You get whatever you expect in life. If you think you'll get burned then, most likely, you will. However, if you believe that you can control the fire or even put it out, then, most likely, you'll succeed.

Of course, everyone worries now and again. Everyone has off days. It's what we humans do, and it's totally normal. The problem occurs when you focus far too much on your worries or the things that stress you out most. I was focused so much on not being lovable that I only managed to prove to myself that it was true. It affected my whole life. How I thought triggered anxieties from the past which just led to more pain and confusion in my life. I thought I was like Humpty Dumpty; I really thought that I was broken to pieces and needed fixing. The trouble with Humpty Dumpty, of course, is that all the king's horses and all the king's men couldn't put him together again. If poor old Humpty had only gone down the route of self-discovery, he would have found that you are not literally broken to pieces and that *you* can put yourself back together again and don't need to call in the cavalry.

There comes a point in life when you have to get a grip and make the decision that enough is enough. Do you want to continue feeling ruled by your adoption and the small scared child within, or do you want to live life from a place of authenticity and love? In Chapter 7 we looked at being authentic and how meditation can help calm the mind so that you tune in to your trueness. You can change how you feel and live a wonderfully happier life as a result. This change has to come from your heart not your head. You see your heart, neuroscience tells us, directly influences your brain. So, if you are trying to change your life from a place of insecurity and fear rather than from a place of love, you're going to be walking up the down escalator! As they say, it's not rocket science. Once you acknowledge and understand that how you think influences how you feel and that in order to feel calm on the outside you first have to be calm on the inside, you can begin to make deep changes to your happiness. So being congruent, coherent, harmonious and consistent with how you think, feel and behave is the key to putting yourself back together. I am not saying here that all the world's wrongs can be righted with meditation or that all your hurts will magically disappear or that the lid on Pandora's box will magically close. However, what I am saying is that there can be a certain kind of beauty and freedom in your life once you pay yourself some proper attention and focus on what you really want.

We hold ourselves more accountable than we do others. You don't allow yourself the love and forgiveness you deserve. And you may not even believe you deserve it in the first place. Staying stuck in your story gives credence to what you've experienced; it helps you to never forget it. It can be like imposing a long-term jail sentence on yourself. But loving and forgiving yourself isn't about forgetting, it's just about letting go of the story that is looping in your head. You have a choice Humpty Dumpty: you can either wait at the foot of the wall in pieces and hope upon hope that someone will put you back together again or you can muster up all your courage and strength and put *yourself* back together again. Your choice!

****

****

I was dripping with anxiety and vulnerability as I arrived at Oxford Street tube station. Today, I was going to meet the son that I had not seen in 24 years. I felt scared, scared of what he'd think about me and what I'd think about him. I wondered if this was how Buntie had felt when we were about to meet. My heart went out to her; I had never given much thought to how she was feeling when we met. I figured I knew how my son might be feeling as an adoptee, since we had that in common. My head was all over the place, thinking, thinking and overthinking.

I was scared and excited. We had gotten to know each other well through emails, but there was still a feeling of trepidation and angst as to what the next few hours would bring. I waited, looking at every young man wondering if he were Chris, looking at their features to see if I recognised myself in any of them. I waited and waited. I'd been early to ensure that I wouldn't miss him.

My mobile phone rang. It was Chris. "Jo, where are you? I'm here."

My heart jumped into my mouth! "I'm here too," I said, looking around for him. My heart was pounding so loud that I was sure the commuters could hear it. We quickly realized were waiting at different exits to the station and laughed at the silliness of it. The ice was broken.

As soon as I saw him, it was like he was that new born baby, my child. A wave of love crashed into me with such force that it was almost unbearable. I swallowed it down, afraid it might put him off. We hugged briefly and went to a local cafe to get acquainted. The funniest thing is that we both pulled out a packet of Marlborough Light cigarettes at the same time. We talked about what else we had in common, like both of us despising bread and butter pudding, which made us laugh. We just stared at each other, embracing that moment of recognition when you see yourself in another. Just as I had once done with Buntie, Chris was searching my face for the similarities between us. Over lunch at Planet Hollywood the waiter asked if we were on a date as we were staring intently at each other absorbing each minute facial detail and recognising ourselves in each other. We laughed out loud, slightly shocked but highly amused, and I proudly announced that, "No, he's my son!"

Whilst I seemed at ease on the surface, inside I was bubbling with untamed emotions. I really didn't want to fall off the wall like Humpty Dumpty, to fracture and disintegrate in front of my son. For years I'd been suppressing the feelings of loss, grief and overwhelming guilt at giving him up. Where were those feelings now? 'They don't just disappear now, do they?' I thought to myself.

****

****

When you embark on a journey of self-discovery, it's a bit like being on a train journey. The speed at which you travel is not always consistent and you might make many stops at stations along the way, some more remote than others. How we sit at each stop and at each speed is entirely dependent on how we experience the journey. For many adoptees (maybe you too) the journey has been troublesome. Perhaps you've had some amazing stops along the way, experiences that you can recount and that make you smile and feel warm and fuzzy inside. On the other hand, you may have had an awful journey, and all that you can really remember is how terrible it's made you feel.

The thing is, wherever you are on that continuum, you can move from where you are emotionally. When I fell apart emotionally it was all consuming; I just couldn't see a way out. My train had derailed. The more I focused on it, the worse it got. I seemed to be frozen in time somehow. There comes a point when the realisation kicks in that life could be different, better even. You have to want it though. You have to want to let go of the stuff that drags you down and have enough belief to make it happen. You can do it. I know you can. I did, and I was my own worst enemy, the instigator and manifester of my own personal bleakness. My coach asked me the probing question, "Do you want to be exactly where you are now, this time next year?"

I replied with a resounding, "No."

Self-Check-In

How much time do you spend thinking about your past versus your future? When you think about your future, do you worry about what might be coming or do you have a clear and positive picture of where you want to go? If you began to devote yourself to focusing on the future, try to imagine what you could achieve.

If you allow yourself to continually run from what you *don't* want to happen you will end up manifesting the very past you fear in your present. You may crumble or even fall apart completely. You may feel like you will never be able to put yourself back together, always being continually broken down by your past like a recurring Humpty Dumpty nightmare. But you do not need all of the king's men to put you back together again, you don't need to keep running from your past, you need only yourself and to trust in your future.

****

****

Chapter 8 Personal Alchemy Exercise Part One

If you have done the exercises in the previous chapters, you should now be more fully tuned in to yourself. You are getting to grips with meditation and calming your mind, have asked yourself some serious questions and worked out how amazing you are. The next step is all about telling yourself a different story without negating the one you already have, forgiving yourself and embracing life more fully on your own terms. In the next chapter, I'll share how you can truly influence how your life pans out in front of you. But for now, here are a couple of exercises that have worked for me to help put myself together again by cultivating gratitude and forgiveness. Do both of them for 30 days and see how you feel afterwards. Set a reminder on your mobile phone so you don't get distracted. One is practiced at night and the other in the morning. It will take you 10 minutes to do each.

Make a gratitude list.

One of the emotions that I learned to cultivate early on in my healing journey was gratitude, the emotion you feel when you are deeply thankful or appreciative about something. It's an emotion that connects you to something greater than yourself. This might be another person or to nature or indeed a higher consciousness.

Making a gratitude list has so many benefits. It can help you feel less stressed. When you start to identify what you feel grateful for in life, it really helps you gain more clarity on what you want and takes your focus away from what you don't want. There are other tangible benefits, too, such as more optimism and more happiness. Gratitude also helps reduce the toxic side effects that you may feel when you are down in the dumps, such as anger and self-deprecation.

Do this before you go to sleep at night, if you can, as it may help you sleep calmly and ensure you wake up in a good mindset.

1. Find a blank page in your journal.

2. Write down 5 - 10 things that you are grateful for. They can be anything you like, maybe your children or spouse, your dog, the sun shining on you, your garden blooming or a film you watched that filled you with joy. Anything you like and are grateful for is perfect. Everyone is different, and your 5 or 10 things will be personal to you.

3. When you write down the words or sentences, try to get a sense of deep appreciation for whatever it is, really feel it.

4. Do this every night for a month, and when you read back over what you've written you will be amazed.

5. If you have a bad day, you can read what you've written and remember that you still have so much to appreciate in your life.

Chapter 8 Personal Alchemy Exercise Part Two

The next exercise is a perfect way to start every morning. Learn from "Ho'oponopono," a very powerful Hawaiian practice of forgiveness that means, "I'm sorry, please forgive me, thank you, I love you."

It is used to help calm disputes, making things right with people and the world. If you want to change the experiences that happen around you, it is first essential to change the experiences inside of you. If you feel fractured, emotionally and spiritually destitute, lost, sad or in any way far from your truth then Ho'oponopono is a wonderful chant to tidy up all that emotional baggage. I now practice this every morning upon waking. At first, I did not realise just how powerful it was, but with time and practice I felt the emotional shifts within. It is an especially useful tool for when you realise that no one else can put you back together again, that task is firmly down to you.

1. Find a quiet space to sit undisturbed and turn off any distractions, like your phone or computer.

2. Softly close your eyes and take a few deep breaths in and out through your nose. Feel your belly rise and fall as you do so.

3. Now say in your mind or aloud, "I'm sorry, please forgive me, thank you, I love you." Repeat this phrase over and over again, as if you are chanting a mantra.

4. You may find that questions pop into your head such as, 'What have I got to be sorry about?' 'Why do I need forgiveness?' 'Who am I thanking and loving?' Don't worry, it is normal, and the more you do it, the more the answers will naturally arise. You will find that 'stuff' from your subconscious mind just floats to the surface. Your subconscious mind is clever and knows exactly where each of the words and intentions are needed.

After a while, when you become more comfortable doing this, you can consciously bring different people to mind when you do this exercise. At times, I thought of my birth mother and other times my adoptive mother. I cried often when things deep within me resonated with the words. I found it hugely cathartic, and I hope it will be the same for you too.

Take out your alchemy journal and write about how you feel after completing these two exercises.

Chapter 9

Who Loves You Baby?

You are Worthy of Love

You can search the entire universe and not find a single being more worthy of love than you. — Gautama Buddha

"What happens if I want to keep the baby?" I enquired, half knowing what answer I'd get.

"You'll have to find somewhere else to live," my mum replied. Those few words penetrated my body and caused a major earthquake. Her voice hit me hard straight in the stomach, and the pain curled around my insides tying a knot in my gut—that hideous feeling totally overwhelming me. It descended over me in an instant, like an unexpected tsunami. A nauseous wave swept over me, and I felt totally out of control of my mind, body and spirit, like I was being buried alive. I felt my subconscious feelings of rejection and

potential abandonment surface. It was as if death itself had called me by name.

I felt crushed, terrified and alone. But I complied. Of course, I did. I always complied. It was my default position from my earliest memories and probably even before then. Comply and obey or face the scolding tongue (or worse) from my mum for not doing so.

It all began when I left college at 17. I was going to become a nurse the following year, but first I decided to take some time out to explore Europe. "You'll need to come back to do your nursing as that will give you a proper job," advised my mum. I could feel her exasperation that I wanted to fly the nest at 17 and have some fun away from home. I think that deep down I wanted to escape from her, to be free to do my own thing and spread my wings of independence. Perhaps learning how to cope with emotionally unavailable parents meant I had developed a deeper sense of adventure. Dad was rather more supportive and said to have fun, do whatever I wanted and have the kind of experiences he wished he'd had at 17.

'Just don't get yourself pregnant,' he said jokingly—famous last words!

I went to Paris to be an au-pair to an American family. Really, I had gone to Paris because I met a boy on a train, but that's for the next book! The city got into my heart and my knickers. I was utterly captivated with her: Paris, the city of love.

I have no idea why I thought that having unprotected sex was a good idea. Well, actually, I didn't. I didn't think about it. I just did it. I needed to feel accepted. I craved attention. I wanted love and connection, and it seemed that there were some who were willing to give it to me.

I went out and partied. I started smoking cigarettes, feeling sophisticated and sexy. I drank beer and smoked cannabis. I flirted outrageously. I always got the attention I wanted, and at times I got more than I'd bargained for. But even that didn't put me off. Nothing could curtail my insatiable desire to feel accepted, to feel loved. A brush with LSD didn't stop me. Even rape didn't stop me. For a few snatched moments here and there, I felt like the centre of another person's world. I felt accepted, wanted and loved. Yet in all this *insanity, I'd forgotten all about accepting and loving myself. I was totally out of love with myself and utterly lost in a vacuum—sucked dry of any emotion. I became a spectator of a story that unfolded before me, in which I, unwittingly, seemed to be the central character. I didn't feel in control; it didn't feel like I was determining how this story would end. I floated through events, disconnected from them, as if watching through frosted glass and not quite being able to make out what was happening. I partied harder and continued falling into a seemingly never-ending void.*

****

****

Have you ever watched someone you love behave so foolishly that you know they will come to some harm sooner or later? You feel powerless to stop them; you want to scream at them to get their attention. You want to yell, "For God's sake, what the hell are you doing to yourself?" But you don't yell at them. You let them carry on even though you know it will all end in tears.

If it is so easy to see this in others, why do we often not notice this behaviour in ourselves? Why do we behave so foolishly at times—so inappropriately, so naively? Why can we not see in advance the damage that we can cause to ourselves and others? We are so blind, becoming lost in our own warped reality, even if that reality is harmful to us. We are totally isolated from love, removed from acknowledging that we are in fact an expression of love ourselves.

There are countless adoptees who are loved so much by their adoptive parents, and they really feel that love inside themselves. It helps them become confident and loving toward others. Conversely, there are still adoptees who grew up in families with emotionally unavailable parents. Maybe this is you? It certainly was me. The net effect of this is that it can impact your own relationships with others and yourself. It can erode your self-esteem and accentuate your fear of rejection and abandonment. Every individual needs love and affection and to be without these basic needs leaves you vulnerable to negative thoughts and an ego that wreaks havoc on your mind. Of course, there are some amazingly resilient adoptees who have become strong, loving and aware of their own patterns and thoughts. But often adoptees can feel emotionally set apart from their adoptive parents. It is essential to feel loved and cared for as a child and young adult as it helps you to form lasting loving relationships with others later in life.

Being separated from your birth mother at such an early age means that you come out into the world with a sense of necessary self-protection that often results in you distancing yourself from anyone that wants to get close to you. It manifests in so many relationships. I know this, because even though I wanted (or indeed craved) to be loved, I pushed people away from me. Many adoptive parents truly believe that if they give their child enough love the child will live out a happily ever after to a (perhaps) tragic story. What many adoptive parents don't understand is that many adoptees cannot actually process, understand or feel the love. Adoptees are paralysed by the fear of not being good enough and not being worthy of love. It doesn't matter if the adoptive placement was amazing or awful. In both cases many adoptees just feel a total lack of self-worth, and the thought of loving oneself is just utter 'hippie shit'.

Every person on the planet needs love, but in order to receive love you first must be totally in love with yourself. Just look at a person who hates themselves. They will find any fault in themselves and will likely avoid being the centre of attention or the life and soul of the party. They are more likely to be sad, lonely and somewhat depressed. That's a sweeping generalisation, but you get my drift. They are less likely to attract love to themselves, are they not? Conversely, look at the person who loves themselves deeply and acknowledges their gifts and amazingness. They will exude confidence, self-worth and love, and they are more likely to take care of themselves. Happy loving people gravitate towards them. Like attracts like. This doesn't necessarily mean to say that anyone who hates themselves isn't capable of seeing love in others. However, it is less likely.

Furthermore, relationships may break down, become strained or not happen at all. There is a highly complex link between how we love ourselves and how others love us. So, for adoptees, the emotional paralysis, which I mentioned before, stops us from loving ourselves and others. It can become so debilitating that it influences our whole perception of the world and our place in it. You have the opportunity to make a choice, you can either explore the gift of self-love or you can remain in denial of it and continue to feel the unwanted feelings that surface and stop you from being in your own truth.

****

****

"Doesn't your mummy love you, poor little thing?" I caught these words being spoken to my baby in the nursery by one of the nurses. I went back to the room and lay on my bed. The familiar feelings of guilt and worthlessness slammed into me. I wanted to defend myself but felt incapable. Inside, I knew I loved my baby. I wasn't giving him up for adoption because I didn't

want or love him. It was because that's how it was, how it had been decided. I needed to tell him, needed him to know that I loved him. I quickly went back to the nursery and picked him out of his cot. "I want you to know I love you; I could never not love you. You will be in my heart. Please forgive me." I looked deep into his beautiful eyes and hoped upon hope that at some level he knew what I was saying. I believed that he did. Even then, as a teenager, I believed that he would know I loved him. He had to know, or I could never live with myself.

My dad had cried when I arrived home from Paris pregnant. His words to me before I left echoed loudly in my head, "Have fun but just don't come back pregnant." I felt a deep sense of shame and guilt knowing that I was the cause of his tears. I sank deep into oblivion; I built up my walls of protection and stayed behind them like a self-imposed jail sentence. At least it meant I was contained and safe. I remained compliant, automatic, devoid of free thought and spent the next few months in a total fog. My mum took control and continually reminded me that I knew adoption was the right thing to do.

"You know babies should have two parents; you know being adopted is a good thing, you have your whole life ahead of you." Her initial response was to ask our family GP for an abortion, but I was too far on in the pregnancy for him to consider it. My mum, a woman unable to have a child naturally herself, and yet she suggested abortion. It didn't feel like she cared, like she loved me or like she would be there when I needed her. She was just so emotionally unavailable. I needed someone to love me, to tell me they loved me and to just hold me. I needed someone to hold me like a mother holds her child, with deep unconditional love. But it never came.

I was sent away to a mother and baby home in Tunbridge Wells. My mum told everyone I was off travelling again—saving face. It was certainly easier for her than telling people that I was pregnant. I felt like a criminal doing time for my sins, and I built my walls higher, thicker, colder. Two weeks after Christmas my water broke as I was in bed. I felt nothing except fear, no sense of expectancy or joy that I was about to bring a new life into the world. I had long since disconnected and I became a watcher in someone else's movie.

"You're giving your baby up for adoption, that's right isn't it Joanna?" asked the nurse after I was wheeled into the hospital delivery room.

"Yes," was all I could reply.

And with that, I was left, abandoned once again, left to my own devices with a head popping around the door every so often to see how I was doing. I was not doing anything. Anything that was 'doing' seemed to be done to someone else. It didn't feel like it was happening to me. It felt like I was an observer in someone else's experience.

"This baby wants to stay in the warm," said the midwife as they decided to hurry things along.

I felt like I was tangled in a black net of guilt. I felt trapped like a caught monster unable to escape. I imagined the muffled voices were talking about me: how I'd gotten pregnant and how shameful that was. I truly hated myself in that moment. And then it was legs up, voices telling me to push, and fear rising in my swollen belly.

"It's a boy, a healthy baby boy," said the doctor. I glanced over and caught a glimpse of a bundle wrapped in blue cotton; I heard him cry out for me before being wheeled out of the delivery room to the nursery. Legs akimbo, I felt exposed and dirty.

A doctor came to stitch me up where they had cut me. He sat at the foot of the bed and talked, looking up through my wide-open legs. I felt vulnerable. He asked how old I was and how come I was having the baby adopted. He seemed to care. I clung to that moment—that bizarre moment with a young doctor sitting at the foot of my bed sewing me up. He stroked me and asked if I could feel anything yet. His stroke felt tender, familiar and inappropriate. I told him that the feeling was coming back. He looked up, patted me, smiled and left. I wanted him to stay with me. I wanted him to talk to me and to tell me everything was going to be okay. I quietly begged him in my head. "Please tell me I'm not a terrible person." He didn't respond. How could he? It was just my thoughts in my head begging him. I felt an emptiness, and in that moment, it was all I had.

For the record, you are worthy, worthy of everything whether it be success, happiness or love. Being in an emotional void, where you are not connected to your inner magic and where you unconsciously feel worthless and unlovable, takes its toll on you. Believe me when I say that your worth and self-love programs are within you; they are just dormant, and you've lost track of them. No one is any less worthy than anyone else, and as soon as you realise that, then you can start to change how you feel about yourself.

It took me years after having my baby adopted before I started to feel good about myself. The old 'I'm worthless' chestnut kept rearing its ugly head. I would blame how I felt not only on being adopted, but also on relinquishing a child. I was so far removed from loving myself that I found it hard to love others and let them love me. I mentioned in Chapter 3 that what we believe to be true and what is actually true are very often not the same thing. At the very heart of our self-esteem lie the core beliefs we have about ourselves. So, the beliefs that you are worthless and unworthy of love can generate overwhelming feelings that penetrate your daily life. You doubt yourself in many situations, blame yourself when things go wrong, focus solely on your weaknesses and allow negative self-talk to rule you. And it's not all in your head. It can become out of control and affect your physiology, too. You feel tired and depressed; you believe that you're just not good enough. I know this all too well, and for many years I was overly sensitive to criticism, not comfortable in relationships, controlling and manipulative and not taking the best care of myself by drinking excessively and smoking weed. I wouldn't acknowledge when I had done things that were successful; I found fault in them and just felt that any praise from others wasn't justified.

Thankfully, after several years of self-discovery and inner work I now love and respect myself. I see myself with all my flaws and accept them. It's incredible, really, how love is so healing. Remember the Beatles song, "All You Need is Love?" Well, in some respects that's absolutely true. Because love is healing, consuming and powerful. Once you realise this and allow love into your life like never before, you can start to live the life you really want.

It's incredible how life can change, how it can get better and how you can feel so much brighter and lighter. What's even more amazing is that other things tend to follow on. Life gets easier, money flows better and relationships improve. I'm not suggesting for a moment that it's easy, that you wave a magic wand and life is perfect. But what I am saying is that once you crack open your heart and start to love yourself as the amazing individual you are, life does get easier. Throughout life, we are all on a voyage of self-discovery. Each day is an opportunity to learn something new. Once you understand that you have the ability to change and acknowledge that the power to do so is right inside you, then you will feel so much better.

Self-Check-In

What have you got to lose by loving yourself and what have you got to gain? When you break it down and ask that question of yourself the answer is straightforward. You have nothing to lose except misery, depression and anxiety. The gains are massive: happiness, gratitude, self-mastery and healing. Who wouldn't want those? You can make the choice right now to love and forgive yourself, to allow your greatness to burst through and to stop the denial of self-love obliterating you.

Learn how to love yourself. *You* are the most important person in your world. So maybe you've had enough of the self-loathing, self-deprecating thoughts and behaviours and now feel that maybe the time is right to try some self-love. Don't be scared. It becomes much easier the more you practice. You deserve your own love. Remember what Martin Luther King Jr said: "I have decided to stick with love as hate is too much of a burden to bear." Loving yourself feels good. Love can heal the deepest of wounds, and you deserve your own love and forgiveness.

****

****

Chapter 9 Personal Alchemy Exercise

This is an exercise that has worked for me and will help you develop your own self-love, writing a love letter to yourself. Take out your journal and write from the heart. It may even help to look at yourself in the mirror for a few minutes or to sit with your hand on your heart connecting to the deeper parts of yourself. The following is a love letter I wrote to myself.

Dear JoJo,

Wow, it's been so long since I really spoke to you, sharing exactly how I feel and reminding you that I love you. For quite some time, I was so wrapped up in negativity that I totally forgot about you. I left you to drown in a sea of emotions and never once threw you a lifeline. I was so lost in the image that I had created of myself that I became removed from you. I didn't take the time to think about how my thoughts and behaviours affected you or how you might feel as a result. I should have been with you through your toughest moments, the times you cried alone, the time your heart felt like it might break. But instead I ignored you and allowed your suffering to continue.

I really need to apologise and tell you, right now, that I love you deeply and sincerely. I love you with my whole being and without any conditions attached. You are so worthy of love. You are amazing. I love you for seeing the good in everyone, for your love of animals and nature, for the way you have mothered your children and for being such a great friend to so many people.

I love seeing the journey of self-discovery that you have been on and that you are finding the best version of yourself possible. It is a joy to behold. You are totally amazing, you really are. Let me tell you that you do not need anyone else to validate you. You do not need to seek approval all the time. You and I are in this life together, and I will be by your side as we go forward from here on out. The past is in the past and together we can create something new and exciting. I value you; I hear you; I see you. I want you to realise that the love I have for you now can never ever be taken from you.

I love you for exactly who you are, right now and always.

I love you so much,

JoJo

Chapter 10

Recognising The Miracle

You are a Miracle

There are only two ways to live your life. One is as though nothing is a miracle. The other is as though everything is. —

Albert Einstein

When I was a small child, I believed that miracles could happen. I read about them in the Bible and learned about them at Sunday school. They were incredible and inexplicable events like healing, walking on water or turning water to wine. I was fascinated with how these miracles could happen. I was blown away when the Bible told us that Jesus made seas calm and made the lame walk and the blind see. It was fascinating to read. Following my confirmation at 11 years old, I thought that since God had made me his own he might grant me a miracle or two.

I had prayed for my own miracle. I prayed that I would find my birth mother and that she would love me. I bargained with God and told him, "I'll be really good if you let me see my real mother." I'd tell God that he could hurt me if I didn't behave or that I would have my babies in pain. If he was all powerful, omnipresent and able to create miracles, then he would surely perform one for me. But he didn't. There was no miraculous happening, no thunder clap with a host of angels descending bringing forth my birth mother to me on a cloud, a bus or any other way. I felt deeply disappointed. Miracles, it seemed, were not for me.

"I don't believe in miracles," I once told a friend at Sunday school when we were listening to the loaves and fishes story for the hundredth time. "They are not real. You can't really feed 5,000 people with 2 loaves and 5 fish." I felt superior; at least I wasn't duped into believing in miraculous happenings any more, even if everyone else seemed to be.

"But it's a miracle. That's the whole point," replied my friend, lapping up the miraculous story like it was the first time she had heard it. I wasn't convinced. I really tried to get my head around it, but it was just too farfetched for my

11-year-old mind. I secretly wanted to believe, and I was still fascinated by the idea of miracles. One of my favourite miracle stories was the Christmas story about the birth of Jesus. The idea of a miracle birth was intriguing to me. It was like magic. That God should be the father to Mary's baby by magic filled me with wonder. It was also a story of adoption, as Joseph was not the birth father. Of course, as a child I had no comprehension of what a virgin birth actually meant, but it all seemed quite straight forward and lovely to me at the time. I liked the baby Jesus in my book. I wondered if he ever felt like me?

"Your mother couldn't look after you and knew that a baby needs two parents," my adoptive mother would tell me. It was her way of justifying my adoption to me. I thought back to the baby Jesus story. He was given up by a parent (his father not his mother) and grew up with two people who loved him. It seemed like it worked for Jesus, so I just accepted it. I wondered who my birth father was. I sometimes wondered if God might be my father. What a miracle that would be!

Miracles are seen as divine interventions in human affairs. I'm not a religious person and do not believe in God in the religious sense. However, the more I delved into my own beliefs around miracles, the more I sensed something way greater than I could even comprehend. I believe we are surrounded by a universal energy that radiates love and connects us to each other. The more I understand this, the deeper my connection to people becomes. As my connection to people deepens, so, too, does my sense of love, and with this love my perception of the world continues to grow and change. Changing my perception of the world helped to shift something within myself, allowing me to both know and love myself much more deeply.

In the beautiful 2014 film *Winter's Tale*, Beverly Penn tells Peter Lake that we are all connected. She says that, "Each baby born carries a miracle inside, a unique purpose, and that miracle is promised to one person and one person alone. We are voyagers set on a course towards destiny, to find the one person our miracle is meant for." I love that! Imagine if this were true, what a journey our life would be as we search out for that one person in order to give them our miracle. Beverley goes on to say, "But be warned: as we seek out the light, darkness gathers and the eternal contest between good and evil is not fought with great armies... But one life at a time." This is such a great metaphor for life. We each travel a road of ups, downs, darkness and light, and yes, it is by our own personal deeds and actions that we can help other people make changes in their lives.

I would like to think that, in fact, we have a bundle of miracles to give to others. Not necessarily humongous miracles but small ones that are hardly even noticeable at first. I imagine a miracle ripple, rather like when you throw a stone into a pond and watch how the ripples spread out with greater diameter. One small act of love and kindness towards one person could be the miracle they need in order to pass it forward to another. However, to recognise the miracle in us and share that miracle, first we must be able to love ourselves without limits. And acceptance of who we are in our entirety is essential if we are to do either.

Loving myself hasn't been easy for me, as I've said in the previous chapter, and I think this is true for many people, not just adoptees. When you feel unworthy of love you become so focused on those feelings of unworthiness that you fail to love others, to accept love from anyone or to even give love to yourself. Feelings of guilt and abandonment cloud our perception and understanding of the world and act as a barrier to love. Many adoptees do not even see the unconscious behaviours that stem from this lack of self-worth and self-love. There are thousands of adoptees across the world who stay stuck in this story, stuck in their victim mode and unable to shift their mindset of being forever unworthy. I don't judge them for this; I just feel a deep empathy for them, as I now know there is a way out of feeling like a victim. If I could wave a wand and work magic for all adoptees, I would make them able to see and feel their own self-worth and recognise that they, too, are amazing miracles.

What is the complete opposite of miracle? Whatever it is, there are many people, adoptees included, who feel like this. They are utterly stuck in their story, which is the antithesis of any miracle. Anytime things in life are challenging or uncomfortable adoptees blame it on being adopted. It helps rationalise things to yourself. Of course, you are only viewing the world through your own skewed filters and not as it actually could be. Life itself is a miracle, and we are each a perfect and unique example of one. Accepting that we are miracles can be challenging, as so many adoptees play out the story of being worthless, unwanted and anything but miraculous. We have a choice to make, as Einstein says. Which will you choose?

For me, my mindset started to change when I began working with my amazing life coach, Brett, who helped me see things from a new perspective. He once said to me, "JoJo, if you don't believe in miracles, just remember that you are one." I'd never really considered myself a miracle, but as I worked with my coach and he helped me understand that my thoughts about myself are not real. And I started to feel a shift inside me. The idea that miracles are all around and that you are one of them might be a new concept, but it's one that you may want to embrace. Everything around us is a miracle—the universe, the planets, our world and life itself. The more we think about the amazing way in which we, as humans, exist, the more we can feel closer to the miracle. The mere fact that your own life is being sustained by your body and that it does this without any prompting is utterly mind blowing. That we can exist on a planet that spins around in space and time and not float off into space is a miracle.

The more I thought about being a miracle the more I felt connected to something far greater. Call it God, call it Source or The Universe. It doesn't really matter, but whatever it is, I felt more connection to it when I looked at myself from this new perspective. It was like being reborn, and you see things like you've never seen before. Flowers look more colourful and trees more vibrant. I began to see how falling snowflakes were so different, unique and intensely beautiful, like the stars in the vast universe twinkling all around us. I realised that miracles are not just about turning water into wine or walking on water; they are not so farfetched and fantastical. Miracles can be everyday occurrences that we have simply forgotten to acknowledge as we got caught up in our humdrum lives. With renewed vision, I saw my own children as precious miracles, each one beautiful and unique. The more I explored the miracles around me and saw the beauty and wonder in everyday things, the more I started to recognise the miracle of me.

****

****

"What does your tattoo say?" My friend asked me.

"Miracle," I replied, "It reminds me that I am a miracle and that life itself is a miracle and that I can be the catalyst for miracles in others." I decided to get my first tattoo in my 50's. I had always been very anti-tattoo, judging those that had them and wondering why on earth anyone would want to mark their bodies in such a way. The change came in 2005, when I was in the Himalayas in Nepal and saw two elderly Nepalese ladies with tattoos on their lower legs.

"What's the significance of those tattoos?" I asked my Nepalese friend. He replied that they were a kind of prayer, and that when the women died the prayers would go up to the universe with the smoke of their funeral pyre. I was moved by this; I loved the idea and decided that at some point I would also have a tattoo with a meaning that could be offered to the universe as a form of prayer.

It took me a while to decide on my first tattoo, and eventually 'Miracle' seemed the most obvious. It would be a constant reminder that I am a miracle. It certainly hurt though! I never expected a miracle to be so painful, *but I guess that, in a way, the discomfort of actually having the word tattooed on my inside forearm was all part of my miraculous journey.*

****

****

To love ourselves without condition means exactly that. We have to love yourselves without conditions attached. There are no ifs, ands or buts; it's all or nothing. We have to be prepared to accept ourselves for the miraculous unique bundle of cells that we are, warts and all. That's not easy, as I've found out. It takes practice, *consistent* practice, even when you feel like shit. It's also something that you have focus on day in and day out because if you don't, and I know this from personal experience, you screw everything up.

It starts with changing the movie that you've been playing on loop inside your head for your whole life, flipping the script, so to speak, and rewriting what's been written. You need to take out the tragic storyline and reword it so that when the movie plays again, it's a much more enjoyable experience. They say each new day is like a blank sheet of paper. You can write whatever you want and create the day you really want, and with each page you can create the life you really want. If it's so simple, why don't people do this? It's hard work—that's why—and it's also bloody scary.

You could start by taking Albert Einstein's quote, from the start of this chapter, to heart and live each day as if everything is a miracle. For some that might seem quite straightforward. However, maybe you just can't make that giant leap from where you currently are. That was me, unable to take the leap. I needed to talk small steps first to lead up to the giant leap. But where to start? I decided to do a SWOT analysis of myself, outlining my strengths, weaknesses, opportunities and threats. This is often employed in business strategies, but it can also be effective for personal use. I highly recommend you do this as well. The results may surprise you.

What are your strengths? For example, what are you great at, what do people you know say about you, how do you show up? You might have words like caring, kind, thoughtful, passionate, helpful, funny, selfless, loving, beautiful, compassionate, trustworthy, friendly or inspiring. Next, you must confront your weaknesses, or at least traits that you currently perceive to be weaknesses, areas in which you talk unkindly to yourself. You might have words like, ugly, short, unlovable, useless, angry, unforgiving, procrastinator, indecisive, manipulative or victim. Look at this list (which I suspect may be much longer than your strengths list) and ask yourself if the words you have used are actually true. Do you truly believe those things about yourself? You can use the exercise in Chapter 3 to help you here. When I seriously asked myself that question, I soon realised that most of what I'd written wasn't true at all. It was grossly exaggerated. I knew they were not true, but the effects of my 'weaknesses' seemed to show up in my life more often than I'd have liked.

Now, move on to opportunities, list your skills, connections, knowledge, motivation or anything else you can think of. You may be surprised. The longer you look at that list, the more opportunities you may realize you have been missing! Next, look at the threats to you achieving your opportunities. When I did this, I found that the biggest threat was *me*! I was in my own way, blocking my every direction and acting as gatekeeper. Fuck! That was the kick in the butt I needed. *I was in my own way*!

Self-Check-In

Look back at your SWOT analysis of yourself and consider the role you yourself have played in the things you may have listed. I would not be the least bit surprised if you come to the same conclusion and find that you, too, are in your own way.

How can you possibly see yourself as a miracle if you keep stopping yourself? As ridiculous as that sounds, it's true for so many adoptees. We get in our own way! We obstruct our happiness and joy and then bemoan anyone who points it out to us or, even worse, tries to help us see a way through. The old defensive ego kicks in, and we put up the barriers. There was one big problem with this realisation: I had no idea how to move myself out of the way. I'd been blocking myself for so long that the very idea of getting out of my own way seemed insurmountable, like climbing a mountain with absolutely no preparation or mountaineering gear. It may seem like an insurmountable task to you, too, but I promise you that it isn't once you know how to approach it.

Blocking your own way, you become your own worst enemy. Curtailing the potential for a better life, fear becomes your driving force. Many adoptees are consistently plagued with the fear of abandonment. It is a deeply rooted subconscious insecurity that we are not really aware of until we start going on an inner journey of self-discovery. This fear surfaces time and time again and can be triggered when we least expect it. For example, in close relationships we can become possessive, but in doing so we ultimately just push others away thus creating the very rejection we fear. We can work ourselves up into such a frenzy about being abandoned that it stops us dead in our tracks, and we end up not moving forward. "What's blocking you moving forward with your life JoJo?" One of my friends asked over coffee one day.

"Well, I realise it's me in my own way" I admitted. She looked at me intently and asked where, exactly, I was blocking myself. I shut my eyes and visualised myself. I saw me standing directly in front of myself.

"What would happen if you just picked yourself up and moved you to the side?" She asked.

"Holy fuck," I screeched. "I can see nothing in my way now!" For such a simple technique the effect was mind-blowing, and I guess I was ready to move myself out of the way. I'll explain this mind-blowing technique at the end of this chapter in the Personal Alchemy Exercise section.

Gradually (and I mean *gradually*) I started to feel a change in myself. I started to connect to my heart rather than my head. I started to change the story of self-deprecation, and what I found was not as terrifying as I was expecting. When you consciously start to change how you see yourself through what you tell yourself, it's like seeing through your own eyes for the first time. First, you start to see the lights and colour, and, eventually, you start to see the awesomeness of the world and its place in the universe. Everything around you is just as it was before, the people, the world and everything in it. The sun and moon still do what they do, the birds still sing, and the grass still grows. However, once you start to feel the change in yourself, the connection to everything else changes with it. You will no longer feel like the scared adopted child inside of you is running your life or that life is happening to you without your knowledge.

Anthony De Mello, in his book *Awareness,* suggests that we filter things out all the time and thus we miss so much. We are so conditioned by society, parents, school and friends that our vision of the world becomes distorted. I most definitely had a distorted view of everything, even though for so long I believed it all to be true. Your adoption, your relationships, the way in which you see yourself and others are often totally warped. You constantly seek validation and approval from people in order to feel compete, to feel that you matter and that you are worth something. I think that this is one of the biggest miracles of all, that moment when you realise that, actually, you didn't need anyone to validate or approve of you. You can chase your fear away, connect to something deeper within you and feel the lead weight lifting off you. It's as if you are performing your own miraculous alchemic transformation, and it feels amazing.

****

****

Chapter 10 Personal Alchemy Exercise

Move yourself out of your own way. Find a quiet space where you can relax. You can be sitting or lying down for this, whichever is more comfortable for you.

1. Focus on your breathing and allow the natural rhythm to flow. Do not force anything.

2. Gently close your eyes.

3. Now, visualise yourself standing in your own way. Where are you? Are you directly in front or to the side?

4. Wherever you see yourself, imagine that you are becoming lighter and lighter, until you can pick yourself up.

5. Now just pick yourself up and move yourself out of the way—really feel yourself doing it (Imagine moving a light cardboard cut-out of you).

6. When you have moved yourself out of the way, visualise the way forward in front of you. Is it clear now? If it is not clear, then what else is blocking your route? If you

need to, repeat this step to move other people or obstacles out of the way until your path is clear.

7. Now that there is nothing else in your way, allow yourself the opportunity to imagine what exciting opportunities are waiting for you down that path.

8. Once you can see the clear path and have imagined what it may hold, open your eyes and just notice how you feel inside.

This exercise was a miraculous revelation for me, one which I still use if ever I get stuck going forward with my life. So, use this exercise to help you live your life like it is a miracle, because it truly is.

Chapter 11

Create Your Blueprint

Design the Life You Really Want

If you don't design your own life plan, chances are you'll fall
into someone else's plan. And guess what they have planned
for you? Not much. — Jim Rohn

"Wow, this place has such an amazing feel to it," I remarked to my Thai
friend as we were driving around the island of Koh Samui in Thailand. I
was attending my friend's transformational yoga and meditation retreat on the
island and had gone off to explore. I'd wanted to leave the UK and all the
heaviness that I felt there to live a simpler life in Asia.

We happened upon a fishing village on the south of the island away from the
tourist spots and traffic. It was early evening and the sunset over the sea was
utterly captivating. "Oh, I could seriously live here," I told my friend. "I'd
love a little Thai house with some land for a dog near the sea with my own

coconut trees," I ruminated. "Actually, just like that old place!" I excitedly shrieked as we turned a corner and drove down a quiet jungle road.

My friend stopped the car. There was a man fixing the barbed wire fence, and she asked him about the place. He said it was available for rent! I couldn't believe it. It was like I had manifested this house as instantly as I had imagined it. I got out of the car for a nosey around the place. It was perfect for me, exactly what I had imagined in my mind less than a minute previously. I was stunned. It needed a jolly good clean, and the garden was a total jungle, but it had all the makings of a place that I would feel happy in.

"I'll take it," I breathlessly exclaimed. Two months' rent up front and that was it! Oh my God, I was going to rent a house in Thailand. I had been talking about spending the winters in Asia for ages. I had talked and talked and talked and talked some more yet every winter I was still in the UK. This time, I had made the effort to visualise what I wanted, recognise it when I saw it and take action to make it my reality.

****

****

When you ditch your labels, open up to allow good things to flow your way and start to love yourself, you may find that life takes on a whole new perspective. Many adoptees are just stuck fast in their story, like pages of a book super glued together. However, with careful peeling apart, you can move on to the next blank page and be confident that your early limitations do not have to determine who you are now or who you will become in the future. Stepping aside from the story in your head and writing a new one is both scary and adventurous. As Shakespeare said, "It is not in the stars to hold our destiny but in ourselves." We really do have that power. You do not have to cling to the past, to feelings or behaviours that drag you down.

Your whole life is governed by your thoughts. They shape and define who we become day in and day out. Earl Nightingale, a US motivational speaker, said that, "We become what we think about." We are the sum-total of all our thoughts. So, it stands to reason that if we have negative thoughts, it will be reflected in our lives. My beautiful daughter, Lucy, offered a great example of this to me. She had recently moved and didn't have a job. She's highly experienced in her field and applied for hundreds of jobs to no avail. She was desperately fed up and would focus her conversations with me on the lack of income and job. I suggested she visualised getting the next job that she was interviewed for, seeing herself in the office with the people doing the work. It was a difficult paradigm shift for her, but she did it and got the job! I'm not saying it's always so quick and easy. But if we get out of our own way more, stop listening to the negative thoughts in our head and get ourselves into a state of allowing things to unfold, then life is so much smoother.

What do you actually want in life? We are all here for such a short time that it makes sense to have the life you want. So, what does that look like for you? Have you ever stopped and asked yourself that question? Why not ask yourself that right now? Everyone dies, but not everyone lives, and I want you to live your life in happiness and joy; you deserve that. It might come as a profound realisation that you become what you think about. It may even touch a raw nerve or make you feel defensive, as if blame is being thrown at you for how you're feeling. No one is throwing blame around (certainly not me). However, you do need to recognise and understand that you have contributed to where you are now. Yes, you didn't choose to be adopted, and I get that. But how you respond now, today, is your choice. Once I accepted that, things changed radically for me, and I believe they will for you too.

You are not your adoption label, your pain, your looks or anything else. If you need help letting go of this, the meditation in Chapter 7 can help you detach from the negative thoughts in your head. Life is a series of choices that can either move you towards something that you really want or keep you stuck in a place you'd rather not be. You don't have to be satisfied with your lot, you really don't. If you can make the connection between how you have been thinking up until now and how your life is currently working out for you, then you can grasp the future and shape it however you want.

What does your current blueprint for life look like? Was it designed by you or someone else? Maybe your adoptive parents mapped out what your life should look like. They did it from a place of love, but it may not necessarily resonate with you now. I'm guessing it's fairly traditional, school, college or university, job, marriage, family, children, success etc. Is this life working out for you the way you once envisaged? If not, then you now have a fantastic opportunity to rewrite your blueprint based on what you really want your life to be like.

I wonder if you have ever asked yourself what matters most to you? It can be bloody hard to determine what you want your future to be like. Chances are you haven't seriously thought about it all. As an adoptee, having a vision can help define who you want to be. It can be the motivating factor that keeps you striving for something better. I never really asked myself that question or, indeed, any questions about what I am capable of or what kind of life I wanted to live. Consequently, for a long time I floated in a bubble of detachment, disconnected from myself and the wider world around me. When you really get to grips with visualising positive things it's incredible, almost magical, how life dances to your tune. So, my next suggestion to you is to create a vision for your life, your new blueprint, something that will fire you up with passion so that it drives you to take action.

Your new beginning starts now. And it all starts in your head, with the way you talk to yourself, the things you do that influence how you feel and the belief that you want something better. You can create a work of art, a beautiful new story that flows with grace and love, a story that means you can live your life from a place of beauty deep inside yourself. Many coaches talk about being your own hero. So be it! You are good enough. You are worthy of love. You are amazing. Life is beautiful, and you are a miracle. What would you look for in a hero? Be that person yourself. You can, you know.

****

****

The idea of moving to Thailand was super exciting and romantic. I had visualised what I wanted, and it had become a reality. However, I was stuck sweating the small stuff and getting flustered about it. Too many 'what if's loomed, and I almost got to the point where my ego had talked me out of going completely. The ego, the voice of sense and survival, was over protecting me, as always. Thoughts about what I was going to do with my belongings, my beloved dog, what my children would say and how I was going to make any money to survive, consumed my waking hours. I realised that I was stopping my own happiness by sweating the small stuff and letting them be the excuses for me not taking action.

I meditated and allowed my intuitive nature to surface, some might call it my higher self or consciousness. It doesn't matter what it's called really, I just allowed it to become stronger than my ego. Instead of focusing on the minute detail, I visualised how I would feel living in the house I had manifested. I felt lighter and clearer and came to decisions that led to action. I did not need to make things complicated. I gave away most of my possessions to charity or family and found a small storage space for the rest. A friend with several dogs offered my dog a home with hers for the rest of his life. I decided not to focus on the lack of money and allow it to flow to me when the time was right. It did. My children were happy for me, my dog settled, my possessions sorted, and bags packed. I was off to Thailand, the land of coconuts and smiles.

On the plane the realisation hit me—I was finally in the driving seat of my life and that I could, with belief, trust, grace and action, have the life I truly wanted and had visualised. Now that I had opened myself up to the possibilities and allowed them to flow to me, my life really became mine. All the work on self-discovery I had done previously, all the coaching and meditation I had done with Brett, the times he had gently but firmly reminded me that I have the power inside me to design and create the life I want, all synchronised in that moment. I cried.

****

****

Make a deal with yourself that you will not stress over the small stuff. We spend so much time worrying about small things that they stop us from getting to the big things. We don't focus on the bigger picture, or we worry about what other people might think. Once you realise that sweating the small stuff is counterproductive to what you really want, then you become more able to respond to life with ease. This was me with my Thailand house. I went through a few weeks back in the UK allowing the small stuff to get in the way, but once I realised this and stepped aside, things became clearer. And the magic started happening. I had visualised this, had looked day and night at pictures on the vision board next to my bed that showed the life I was expecting to live. I now realise that most things in life are the small stuff and to truly design the life I want, I just need to go with the flow. Or indeed, go with my flow. Easier said than done, of course, as you always come up against resistance of some sort, but once you refocus your energy on the things that you can change and learn to cope with the things you cannot, life gets easier. Life is actually easy. I don't mean to sound glib here, but it really is. When it's all boiled down, life flows with ease. Just look around in nature. You don't see the birds or animals or plants sweating the small stuff, do you? No, they just go with the flow of the planet.

Self-Check-In

What are you really happy with right now? Think about it for moment. Why are you happy with that area of your life? Your blueprint for life is just the story or belief about how your life should be. Being happy in any area of your life usually means you are meeting your life expectations. What about an area in your life you are not happy with? Maybe your adoption story, your finances, relationships or work. Why are you not happy with that area?

When you are not happy, it seems easy to become motivated by fear, fear that immobilises you and ultimately makes you believe that you cannot change things. It can seem so much easier to have negative thoughts rather than positive loving thoughts. But if you allow fear to control your life it takes a strong hold, feeds the ego and convinces you that you cannot change. Therefore, you do not change.

But by now, hopefully, you have realised that these negative thoughts do not have to define who you are in the present. These thoughts are like all those small things. Though they may seem insurmountable, if you can focus on designing your blueprint, that vision you have for what your life could be, the small things will melt away. You do not need to hang on to old paradigms and beliefs that serve no purpose and make you feel like shit. They will pop up in your head, but you have the tools to deal with them. Your next page is blank, and this gives you a wonderful opportunity to design your own blueprint for life. It's not anyone else's—it's yours, and it can be designed purely on what you want to achieve in life. A blueprint for life is rather like an architect's drawing of a new building. Imagine yourself as a grand design and make sure that you have firm foundations and a solid belief in going forward. Do not let anything or anyone get in the way of that, including yourself.

****

****

Chapter 11 Personal Alchemy Exercise

I have found that visualising things and using a vision board are both super helpful. Not everyone can easily visualise their desires, I know that, and so using a vision board is a great way to emphasise what you want in a tangible way. I have personally found the process of developing a vision board both immensely satisfying and deeply meaningful. It seems to me that many people don't seriously imagine in their mind's eye what their ideal future looks like. Most people think it's some sort of 'hippy-happy-clappy' nonsense, that it's a total waste of time. Nevertheless, what I have learned on my own journey is that visualising or, at the very least, having a vision for your life, can dramatically impact how your future pans out. Having a big picture of your life can help define your raison d'être, your 'big why'. Our brains are cluttered and become easily distracted, so a specific vision can bring mental clarity. It helps you focus on where you are heading, and it brings life to the smaller action steps you need to take that will lead to your vision. Vision without specific action is just a dream. You have to take action to make the vision a reality but having the vision in place is the first practical step.

Use this practical exercise below to create a vision board and see how that helps your life move forward.

What you will need:

A large sheet of plain paper (I used A3 size) or a large piece of board that you can embellish

Glue

Scissors

A pile of magazines or a computer and printer

A few pens

A clip frame (if you want to frame the vision board afterwards)

1. Find a quiet spot where you can connect to your deepest thoughts and ideas.

2. Sit comfortably, close your eyes and take five deep breaths. Feel your stomach rise and fall and imagine the air going in and out. With your eyes still closed, allow yourself to relax and tune in to your mind's eye. Do not worry if random thoughts pop up (they will). Just let these thoughts come and go.

3. Ask yourself what you really want your life to look like, both now and in the future. Think about different areas of your life, for example, where you live, your health, your relationships, your finances, your time and how you use it or any of the other things that you care about in the world.

4. Once you have gathered your thoughts, begin to look through the magazines or print off pictures that match the ideas in your head. It may be a dream house or car or maybe pictures that express the joy and freedom you want to feel. Maybe it is a bowl of fruit to represent healthy eating or pictures of someone doing yoga. Perhaps it is finding your birth records or meeting your birth family. Whatever pictures work for you are just perfect.

5. If it appeals to you, write some motivational or inspirational words and quotes on the board too. Next, add some "I am" statements such as, "I am happy," "I am amazing," "I am successful," or "I am proud for doing this."

6. Add your favourite happy photo of yourself to the board.

7. As you cut out the pictures, feel the emotions they represent as if they have already been fulfilled. Spend quality time doing this; it is a powerful process. Connect deeper to the emotions so that you really, truly feel them.

8. Now arrange them on the paper or board in a way that feels good to you. As you place each photo touch it and internalise the future it represents. Read your written words aloud.

9. When you are happy with how the pictures are arranged, glue them into place. Now you can frame it if you want to or leave the board as it is.

Place your vision board right next to your bed so you can see it, morning and night. What you see for the last 45 minutes before sleep replays in your subconscious mind all night. What you see first thing in the morning helps to raise your vibration and, therefore, your mood. Look at your vision board daily, making it part of your morning and evening routines. See and feel yourself living it. Believe that all those things are already yours. Be grateful for what is already in your life. As time goes forward, acknowledge any goals already achieved and any changes you have noticed. Maybe put a tick or heart next to anything on your board that is now part of your current reality. Acknowledge that there is something bigger than yourself at work, even if you may not even know or understand what that is.

If you actually do this and make the effort to look at your vision board day and night, you will (even unconsciously) work towards it. That in itself might be good enough for some people. However, for the vision to really become the reality you absolutely must take some action to make it happen. Having a vision is (I have learned) one of the most powerful things you can do, and it has always kept me focused on what I want. Take this book for example. I told people for years I was writing book. I even had a picture of a book and the words *bestselling author* on my vision board! I looked at it day and night and yes, I took action and started to write. Then I stopped, then started, then doubted, then started again and stopped again. I got nowhere fast. However, once I decided to really buckle down I took the action that my coach suggested and broke the book down into manageable pieces. I set myself a daily target to write for a couple of hours every morning, and this book is the result! If I had not taken the action and focused, my mind would still be cluttered with ideas about writing it and nothing to show for it. Envisioning works, just as long as there is action alongside it.

Chapter 12

Adoption Alchemy

Personal Transformation, and the

Art of Inner Magic

An alchemist is one who transforms everything with love. —
Emmanuel Dagher

"You've been standing in a pile of poo for a long time Jo," one of my good friends highlighted to me. It was true, I had. I'd allowed my story to define me. I allowed my behaviour to be driven by a controlling little girl. I behaved like a child and not an adult. It was time to grow up!

The alchemy really started for me the moment I decided that enough was enough. By doing the same old shit year in and year out, I was getting the same returns. When I really started to unpack myself, what really makes me tick, what screws me up and why I kept beating myself around the head, I came to a realisation. I could either wake up or shut up! I decided to wake up. It seemed a much more adventurous option, scary as hell, but adventurous nonetheless. I had been in the comfort zone of my life for far too long. I had been wearing a lead cloak long enough; I wanted to wear gold, be seen, be real, to shine and be amazing. I knew other people who were amazing and who had been through their own alchemic journey. So why not me too?

Something deep inside me was crying out for change. I had been coached by my friend and attended some transformational retreats. These things were the catalysts I needed to jumpstart my transmutation. Whilst at times I really wanted someone to wave a magic wand and perform a miracle for me, it was abundantly clear that I had all the tools needed in order to change myself. I just needed to put in the work.

I think initially there was a real sense of fear. Not the kind of fear you'd feel if confronted by a man-eating tiger but the negative fear of 'what if', fear of failure and fear of insecurity. It's totally irrational. I get that now, but at the time it was a huge block to me changing the way I felt and unlocking my inner truth. I felt vulnerable at the thought of having to take control of myself, the thoughts and behaviours that had dominated my life up until that point. I hated feeling vulnerable. It reminded me of times past when I truly believed that vulnerability was a sign of weakness. Weakness to me, in those times, meant I was worth less than everyone else. It meant I was unable to cope, and I desperately needed to prove to everyone (including myself) that no matter what life might throw at me I was a coper. I could manage everything on my own and thanks but no thanks if you think I need your help. You see, us adoptees learn some very exotic coping strategies when we are torn from our birth families, and these strategies keep us safe into adulthood. However, this is only a false sense of security, a total illusion about what is meant by being safe and secure. It took a long time for me to realise how far off point I really was.

Once I'd moved myself out of the way, the path forward was much clearer. I knew that there would always be opportunities to stray off at any given point on the journey, but I could still see the path. I guess that's how life is, really. We can be merrily trotting down the road and come to a fork where we need to decide which is the best route to take. Sometimes, it's an utter shit route, and at other times, it's a superb well-paved road. So, it was with my alchemic process. Not as straightforward as just following the yellow brick road but equally interesting and colourful. My journey felt like it was really just beginning and yet I stopped and looked back at how far I had already travelled. Without really realising it, I had travelled quite far already and had just never really given myself credit for it: coping with the knowledge of being adopted, the product of rape, growing up in a dysfunctional family, relinquishing my first child from a teenage pregnancy, being reunited with my birth mother and later my son, being a parent to James and Lucy, facing depression, divorcing, moving away from everyone I knew and starting a new life.

The list seems pervasive, but it's not there to elicit sympathy. It is merely to acknowledge that even though the shit hit the fan on several occasions, I have, as many adoptees do, an internal resilience and strength to keep on keeping on. It was now time to unpack that heavy bag I'd been lugging around and dispose of the things in it that really were no good to me. I'd had enough of the stop/start/stop/start approach to life. It was time to step it up. But where to begin?

****

****

Once you move yourself out of the way (Chapter 10) and delve a bit deeper into how you talk to and treat yourself and others, we can start to work on building yourself back up to where you want to be. And it will become abundantly clear that there are two fundamental things you'll need to address. The first is the common compulsion to apologize for everything and anything. I was always saying sorry, and in doing so I disempowered myself and thus never got to where I wanted to be in life. Like many people, I had no clue where I wanted to be in the first place. I was on a journey with no particular destination, constantly finding fault in myself and apologizing at any given moment. Happiness is a vehicle to get you to your destination of unconditional self-love, and this journey can be derailed by those constant apologies. For many adoptees the need to say sorry happens along every step of the journey.

Do you apologise at every opportunity. Do you really have to apologise for everything and anything? It's like you are apologising for everything that is wrong in the world like it's your fault. In the past, I have often felt that things totally beyond my control were my fault. For example, my daughter once got burgled when she was living in London and I automatically felt that it was my fault. If I hadn't divorced several years beforehand then she would still be living at home with me and therefore not in the home that was burgled. Irrational, I know, but that's genuinely what I felt inside. On that day, I rushed the 100 miles in my car, breaking the speed limit, to be with her and the first words out of my mouth were, "I'm so sorry, darling."

Why was I sorry? After all it wasn't my fault, was it? Maybe you're like I was, with an inherent need to apologise all the time, even if it wasn't meaningful. I think it's because, like many adoptees, I was apologising for my existence, apologizing for being who I am. Why, as an adoptee, do you need to allow yourself to feel inferior? I'd suggest it is because adoptees often have such low self-worth that we treat ourselves badly, so badly that, at times, we often don't believe we have any true value. We apologise to defend ourselves, a kind of pre-emptive strike that ensures we don't have to face rejection. But in doing so I was really just giving others permission not to take me seriously. Why would anyone listen to me if I have to apologise before I speak?

I apologised so much that more often than not I would start a sentence with the word 'sorry'. Adoptees excel at this type of self-deprecating behaviour. In fact, we are the kings and queens of it. Think about how often you say 'sorry' in a single day. I was staggered when I did this for a day. I counted every sorry and there were a lot! It trips off the tongue so easily doesn't it? It becomes your mantra to diffuse any further dialogue. Saying 'sorry' ensures that you remain compliant and stops you from feeling rejected. What you don't understand, though, is that the constant need to say 'sorry' leaves a residual effect in you. Being 'sorry' flows through your whole body like a raging torrent. Saying sorry undermines who you are and erodes your self-esteem, and you end up feeling sorry for yourself more than anything else.

True, deeply heartfelt apologies are so different from the superficial 'sorry' that we often say. The true apology comes from those who are filled with honesty and integrity, and whilst we adoptees will often fall into that category, there is a fine line between your need to say sorry in order to defuse attention and to say sorry as an act of real humility. There is a kind of strength that is needed to say sorry and genuinely admit a wrongdoing. In my rampant over usage of the word 'sorry', I had diluted its value to such an extent that some people may not have believed my sincerity. In the past I have said sorry to people who responded by saying: "Yes, but you don't mean it."

Self-Check-In

How often do you use these 'sorry's?

- "Sorry to bother you."

- "Sorry, do you have a minute?"

- "Sorry I missed that, what did you say?"

- Saying sorry when you hit the ball out of court.

- Saying sorry if you bump into someone in the street or if you accidentally push in front of someone in the queue at the supermarket.

- Saying sorry when you make a minor mistake.

What's with all the 'sorry's? It is a total knee jerk reaction. Do you need to be forgiven for living? Of course, you don't. Over apologising is not very glamorous at all. It often just adds fuel to a fire. It makes other people feel that they need to forgive us, but for what? We haven't done anything wrong. It is all rather ridiculous. I love this quote by RM Drake: "One day we'll finally learn to love ourselves and stop apologising for the things that make us who we are."

By now if you've worked through the previous exercises, you will hopefully have started to change how you feel about yourself. You will recognise that you are an amazing human rather than the self-loathing person you may have felt like previously. You know that you are not your negative thoughts and that through intention, visualisation and action you can step into love and create the life you want. You will, I hope and suspect, be in a place where you do not want to remain doing the same old things that make you feel like every day is a bad day. You will want to release yourself from your personal bondage, your own personal *Groundhog Day*, and grasp life by the balls, saying, "Hell yes!" to life and never apologizing for it. You can regenerate yourself, or, as I like to think, perform your own personal alchemy.

****

****

I decided to read Rhonda Byrne's book The Secret, *which is built around the Bible quote, "And all things, whatsoever ye shall ask in prayer, believing, ye shall receive." It talked about focusing daily on being grateful for the things in your life and the idea that you can really create your own reality if you shift your thinking. This helped me to realise that even though I'd experienced a range of traumas, emotional upheavals and self-limiting beliefs, my world had never actually ended, and I was still a functioning human being (albeit a bit of a screwed up one). I started to believe that there was something bigger than me that I could tap into, and that if I worked at it, I could, as others around me had, change my whole life.*

It was like opening the door to a new and potentially enthralling alternative reality. When I think back to my childhood and how I once dreamt of an alternative reality with a different me, I was obviously much nearer to this concept than I had previously realised. The road map of my life to date was built entirely on what I perceived to be true, and, as I had discovered, my idea of truth had become somewhat warped. Everything in life is based on what someone has thought. My life became what I thought about. So, when I focused on how terrible I felt, I felt more terrible. When I focused on having no money, no money came to me. When I focused on anything from a perspective of lack, that is exactly what I got. It's not rocket science to see that if we change our beliefs, we change our circumstances. I came to the realisation that in order to create the life that I wanted, that makes me buzz with imploding excitement spilling into my life and others, I had to put myself first, take care of myself and be happy with myself. I decided not to take things so damn seriously. Life is a game, and once we know how to play it, we can win.

My coach once said that, "You have to be selfish to become selfless." I now understood what he meant. The word selfish has such awful connotations and conjures up greed and self-centred arrogance. So being told to be selfish sort of stuck in the throat a bit. Until, that is, the lightbulb moment came, and I understood that in order to be the change I want to see in the world (to paraphrase Gandhi's quote) I needed to concentrate on my own health and wellbeing so that I was stronger, more resilient and could give myself to others. I was so influenced and moulded by other people's expectations that I had been conforming to their ideals, and, in the end, I lost myself. For years, I was stuck in negative thoughts that served me no purpose whatsoever and just kept me in a place where everyone else was able to suck the life-blood out of me. I stumbled around being all things to all people, losing myself. I was unfulfilled. Yet I continued to give and give, expecting that the rewards would make me feel better, only they never did. In order to really help others, I needed to be coming from my authentic self, but along the way I had lost her.

The more I become selfish, or self-centric, the more I have the capacity to empathise with others. I have always had an overwhelming desire to make things better for people and now instead of doing that from a position of weakness, I am approaching it from a more robust position and finding that the knock on effect is much more powerful. I believe that the choices I make now have the power to change the world. The decisions I make today impact not just myself but the world around me, too. That, my readers, is alchemy.

****

****

So the second fundamental thing that must be addressed in order to rework your relationship with yourself is for you to become more selfish. There is a great difference between giving oneself to others, draining your own resilience, and giving to others from a position of strength, empowering both yourself and others. The latter is far more appealing, and we are much more able to give of ourselves and really empower others if we first cultivate strength within us. I know that it can be both emotionally, mentally and spiritually draining if we help others when we are not in the strongest most resilient frame of mind. You may think this is just common sense. Of course, it is. However, putting it into practice is another thing altogether. How do you make that shift from self-deprecation to self-appreciation? What magic needs to take place for that to happen? This whole book, if you've read it from the beginning, is a personal alchemic journey. Alchemy, I believe, is a process of change in which we deconstruct ourselves, our stories and our beliefs and put them back together again in a more positive and holistic way. It is a creative, even poetic process like a sea becoming inexplicably calm after a raging storm. Change is scary; change is challenging. Yet change can also be powerful and liberating.

If you think for a moment of some modern change-makers, who springs to mind? Gandhi, Nelson Mandela, Martin Luther King, etc. They all had some qualities in common. They were people friendly, self-motivated, passionate, they understood themselves and the world around them. They knew that they could make a difference. It was Gandhi who first said, "We must be the change we wish to see." He was speaking after a prayer meeting in India, and people kept saying to him that the world had to change for people to change. Gandhi replied that the world will not change unless people change. We are always looking for others to blame for everything that happens; it is never our fault. As adoptees, we are constantly blaming others for how we feel. Gandhi implied that we are each as much at fault as the next person, and unless we change ourselves and help others to change, nobody will change. We will always be waiting for someone else to make the first move. Instead of expecting everyone else to change, you have to take responsibility for your own life and decisions.

You might think the road ahead seems awfully boring. It might even seem like you can't see that far in front of you yet. But if you actually stop and take stock of where you've come from (even since the first few pages of this book) and what is around you, you may realise how far you have already made it. You only need to focus on the one or two steps in front of you for now, not the whole damn journey. Glance back and see just how far you've come. Well done, you have moved in the right direction. The universe has our backs it seems, and we ought to be grateful for that.

I now believe that nothing happens randomly. There is an apparent order in what appears to be chaos. The only true chaos is caused by us, as individuals. I caused my own chaos. You cause your own chaos too, not through any direct conscious decisions but by allowing your ego to control your life whilst trying to defend you. It thought it was doing a good job protecting you. But it was a bit of a 'job's worth', overdoing it and becoming an irritating little bugger. You can tame the ego and move towards your individual vision. You do have to work at it, though. You have to fall down seven times and get up eight. Remember that the past is not the present. You can do nothing at all about it now; it only exists in your mind. We hang on to our shit, going over it time and time again, reliving it like it is the present. I know, I've spent over 50 years hanging on to it! But it is not now. Now is the single moment that you are in, and then that moment becomes the past too. What you focus on you feel, so choose to focus on something good that makes you happy rather than something that makes you sad. Little by little, you will get hooked and reeled in by that happiness, and the sadness will fade. You will find your own inner magic and it totally rocks!

Your Personal Transmutation

- Understand your world. That means understanding yourself better, how you behave and make your choices, and understanding the things that influence your behaviour, attitudes and decision making. It is also about education. You need to educate yourself in order to make informed choices. Read more self-development books and get to grips with the Universal laws that affect us all.

- Align your purpose. This is where you follow your true path and do that which fills you with passion. I had always wanted to help other people feel good. So, I did some coach training to help me help others. And it actually helped me too. What is your purpose?

- Learn to accept that you are fully responsible for your own life and become confident in living towards your full potential. Ask yourself, "Can my purpose be for the greater good?" "If I can find solutions to my own problems then can I use that experience in the world to help others?"

- You have to be the change you want to see. Knowing your place in the world and understanding and accepting responsibility for yourself, you can now start to transform yourself and the environment around you. Then you can move forward to transform the world.

- Let go of indecision. It robs you of your opportunities, really it does. When you decide to decide, the opportunities are limitless. Lead becomes gold, and you can change your life forever.

Once you realise that you are repeating patterns of behaviour year in and year out, often getting nowhere, it can lead to a revelation that can truly transform your life. You have reached the end of this book, but in a way, this is really a beginning. Once you embark on the journey of self-discovery and awareness, you cannot go back to sleepwalking your way through life. I hope that my own personal alchemy has inspired you to take some action to create your own. You now know that what you believe affects how your reality manifests and that changing your beliefs can dramatically change your world.

The mere fact that you have read this far suggests to me that you are already starting to see your own unique truth. You have an amazing journey still to come. You are a wonderful miracle, and I applaud you for sticking with me. Writing this book has been a journey for me, and I hope that the truths, exercises and comments continue to inspire those of you that have been affected by adoption.

I appreciate you greatly.

With Love,

JoJo

Printed in Great Britain
by Amazon